Lifestyle

English for work, socializing & travel

Intermediate Workbook

WITHDRAWN

Louis Harrison

D1347964

PEARSON
Longman

Contents

1

A Tense review
B Present tense question forms
C Free-time activities
D **Communication strategies** Making suggestions
E **Interaction** Life coaching

Quality time

A Tense review

1 Quickly read the article opposite and find these numbers and dates.

1 Janet's age when she stopped working as a dancer _____

2 how long the fitness training takes _____

3 when she opened her first gym _____

4 how many gyms there are now _____

5 how long her working week is _____

2 Read the text again and answer these questions.

1 What was Janet's first job? _____

2 How often does she go to the gym? _____

3 What has taken up Janet's time recently? _____

4 What is Janet planning with *Hips*? _____

5 What does she enjoy after work? _____

3 Complete these sentences about Janet's day. Use present simple, present continuous, present perfect, past simple, past continuous or future forms.

1 Her first job was as a dancer but she *hasn't danced* for four years (not dance).

2 In America she _____ (travel) and working when she saw *Hips* gym.

3 Busy women _____ to *Hips* gym for a 45-minute training session. (go)

4 Before she started her business she _____ any business experience. (not have)

5 Since 2006 she _____ three more gyms in different cities. (open)

6 Now Janet _____ to increase the number of gyms she has. (plan)

7 Last year she _____ a lot about business. (learn)

8 In addition to managing her business, Janet _____ future events for charity. (organize)

9 Although she works hard, she _____ about how many hours she does. (not think)

10 In the next few years Janet _____ a businesswoman to watch. (be)

MY WORKING WEEK …

Janet Douglas
is the managing director of a growing gym operation

Fitness has always been a big part of Janet Douglas's life. She started work as a professional dancer but stopped performing at the age of 25. When she was travelling and working in America she found a gym-franchise called *Hips*, a female-only gym that offers a 45-minute fitness-training course for women with busy lives. When she started her business in the UK, she had no business experience at all, yet she became an overnight success. She opened her first gym in 2006 and she has opened three more sites since then in cities in Britain. 'People like the gyms and they also help raise awareness of fitness in the towns where they operate,' says Douglas. As well as managing her gyms, she too goes to the gym twice a week.

Last year was a big learning curve for Janet and planning and strategy have taken up a lot of her time as she is aiming to expand her gyms to more cities in Britain. Recently, publicity and marketing have occupied her time. She's also planning various charity events in which *Hips* is involved next year. After work Janet enjoys spending time with friends. Although her working week can be around 40 or 50 hours, she's not counting the hours, 'I've never thought about how many hours I work. I just do what I need to do.' Janet is going to be a person to watch over the next few years.

1 Look at this information about a radio phone-in programme and choose the correct topic.

a Making time for yourself

b How to get promotion

c Women in the workplace

> In today's episode of *The Breakfast Show*,
> Deborah Singh talks to Serge Taylor about how
> to include ourselves in the work–life balance.
> Serge asks: ¹◯ **What are the most important
> things in our lives?** ²◯ **Why are you neglecting
> yourself?** ³◯ **What am I doing for myself today?**
> ⁴◯ **Where am I going today?** and ⁵◯ **Is there
> enough room in your life for these choices?**
> Listen between 7 and 9 today for the answers.

2))) **1** Listen and tick (✓) the questions in the text that Serge asks.

3 Listen again and choose the correct answers.

1 Serge says that _____ are the most important things in our lives.

  a rest and relaxation

  b food and drink

  c work and family

2 When you are planning your day it's good to ask _____ .

  a 'What does my boss want today?'

  b 'What am I doing for myself?'

  c 'When is my first meeting?'

3 Focusing on yourself is about _____ . (two answers)

  a taking breaks

  b doing jobs you enjoy

  c doing yoga

4 Look at the questions in exercise 1 again and write present simple or present continuous.

question 1 _present simple_   question 4 _____
question 2 _____   question 5 _____
question 3 _____

5 Put the adverbs of frequency into the sentences. Remember, adverbs of frequency usually go before the main verb but after *be*.

1 It is work and family. (usually) _It's usually work and family._

2 I'm busy taking calls. (normally) _____

3 When we ignore important needs, it makes our performance poorer. (often / usually) _____
_____

4 But remember you're important too. (always) _____
_____

5 The answer is simple. (often) _____

6 Leave yourself out of the process. (never) _____
_____

6 Complete this conversation. Use the verbs in brackets in the present simple or continuous.

Imran: Hi, ¹___*is*___ that Janet *speaking*? (speak)

Janet: Yes.

Imran: Hi, it's Imran. Look I ²_____ (come) into the office but I'm afraid I'm late.

Janet: Oh no, what ³_____ ? (happen)

Imran: The traffic's really terrible – ⁴_____ (be) it usually this bad on Uxbridge Road? ⁵_____ the traffic always _____ (move) this slowly?

Janet: Oh no. On the radio, the traffic report said that they ⁶_____ (work) on the road. ⁷_____ the road works _____ (cause) long delays?

Imran: Yes, I think so. I usually ⁸_____ (try) to listen to the traffic reports before I travel. ⁹_____ you _____ (know) what? Today I didn't do it.

Janet: Oh dear.

Imran: Janet, ¹⁰_____ (be) there a meeting with Geoff today?

Janet: Yes, there is. ¹¹_____ you _____ (try) to be here for it?

Imran: Yes, but I think I'll be late. Can you let him know that I ¹²_____ (wait) still _____ at the traffic lights, but I ¹³_____ (hope) to be there soon. ¹⁴_____ he (stay) _____ for one or two hours after the meeting?

Janet: Yes, I think so.

Imran: Thanks, Janet. See you soon.

1 Look at the advertisements and write where you can do these activities: at Extreme Fitness Camp (EFC) or at Alpine Activity Centre (AAC).

1 football ___AAC___

2 skiing _____

3 massage _____

4 boxing _____

5 mountain biking _____

6 aerobics _____

7 yoga _____

8 hill walking _____

2 Read the advertisements again and underline words that mean the following.

1 very exciting _____

2 very attractive or impressive (2 words) _____ , _____

3 very good (2 words) _____ , _____

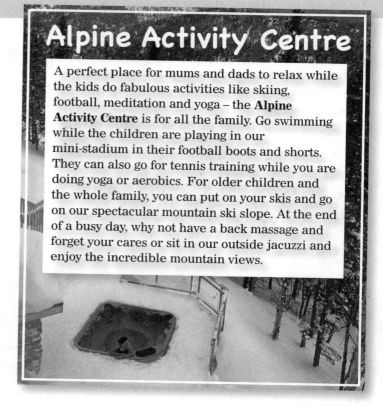

Alpine Activity Centre

A perfect place for mums and dads to relax while the kids do fabulous activities like skiing, football, meditation and yoga – the **Alpine Activity Centre** is for all the family. Go swimming while the children are playing in our mini-stadium in their football boots and shorts. They can also go for tennis training while you are doing yoga or aerobics. For older children and the whole family, you can put on your skis and go on our spectacular mountain ski slope. At the end of a busy day, why not have a back massage and forget your cares or sit in our outside jacuzzi and enjoy the incredible mountain views.

Extreme Fitness Camp

Losing weight and increasing your fitness levels can be difficult and boring. **Extreme Fitness Camp** is an exhilarating way of making exercise and healthy eating part of your life. Each day includes some of the following activities: boxing, aerobics, yoga, hill walking, swimming, and cycling. Cycling and hill walking are in the stunning hills around the camp. You can ride mountain bikes through the forest but you must wear helmets and gloves for safety. Remember, this is a fitness camp, not a health farm – it's amazing fun with incredible results!

3 Look at these underlined words from the advertisements and label them. Use one of the options a–c.

a part of a continuous verb form

b an adjective

c a gerund

1 Losing weight and increasing your fitness levels can be difficult and boring.   (c)(◯)

2 Boot Camp is an exhilarating way ...   (◯)

3 Cycling and hill walking are in the stunning hills ...   (◯)(◯)(◯)

4 ... while the children are playing in our mini-stadium ...   (◯)

5 ... you are sitting in our outside jacuzzi ...   (◯)

4 Put the activities into the table.

~~tennis~~ cycling video games crossword puzzles sudoku puzzles walking skiing yoga boxing aerobics badminton swimming

play	tennis			
go				
do				

1 Complete the sentences below. Use the correct form of the verbs in this box.

> submit   have   come up with
> generate   share   run out of

1 OK, the purpose of this meeting is to _____ ideas for improving communications in the company.

2 _____ anyone got anymore good ideas they would like to _____ with us?

3 Thanks very much, that was a good discussion, we've _____ quite a few ideas today.

4 The deadline to _____ your ideas in writing is 10 January.

5 I'm sorry, I just don't know what's wrong with your PC – I've _____ of ideas.

2))) **2** Listen to a conversation about team building and look at the pictures. Tick (✓) the activities they suggest.

3 Complete the sentences. Use the prompts in brackets.

1 Bai Meng, (what/suggest) _____ ?

2 Wait a minute – (why/we/think/it) _____ first?

3 Perhaps (we/consider) _____ in more detail.

4 (maybe/we/look) _____ the other options.

5 (how/have) _____ a dinner party?

6 (could/take) _____ a bit more seriously?

7 (sounds/to) _____ me.

8 I (think/brilliant) _____ idea.

4 Listen again and check your answers.

5 Are these sentences correct (✓) or incorrect (✗)?

1 Galina has recommended increasing the working hours by 15 minutes each day. ◯

2 If Wednesday is fine with everyone, I propose to meeting then. ◯

3 Didn't Nadira suggest to see a film next week? ◯

4 The recommendations that are being proposed suggest that we need to rethink our marketing strategy. ◯

5 What do you recommend to have from the menu this evening? ◯

6 They are proposing that the company changes its logo to the new design. ◯

⚠️ *Propose, recommend, suggest* are all verbs that are formal and more common in written than spoken English.
*I **propose** we delay the site launch by another month.* (written)
What about delaying the site launch by another month? (spoken)

6 Correct the sentences from exercise 5 that are wrong.

1 Look at the article below and match these figures with the activities.

1 44%
2 2.09
3 23%
4 6.8%

a talking to colleagues
b doing personal business
c surfing the internet
d working hours lost per day

2 Read the article. Are these sentences true (T) or false (F)?

1 Americans mainly waste time at work by surfing the Internet. ☑ T

2 It is difficult to separate work and personal time. ☐

3 The American working day is becoming shorter. ☐

4 Employers want their workers to rest at home after work. ☐

5 Workers are using work time to pay their bills. ☐

6 Reading an online newspaper at work is a waste of time. ☐

3 Look at the article again. Label these activities Timewasting (TW) or Creative waste (CW).

a reading online newspapers _____

b surfing the internet _____

c paying bills _____

d generating new ideas _____

e socializing with co-workers _____

4 Look at the definitions and complete this crossword with words from the article.

[Crossword grid with 2 Across showing: l a c k]

Across

2 when there is not enough of something, or none at all

4 very great tiredness

5 the fact of being unable to do something

6 to make a process or activity stop temporarily

Down

1 delaying doing something that you ought to do, usually because you do not want to do it

3 to put several things or problems in order of importance so that you can deal with the most important ones first

Wasting time productively

A happy worker is a productive worker but does that mean we should socialize at work? A survey found that personal Internet surfing was the top method of procrastination in the office for 44% of people; the average worker wastes 2.09 hours per day on this. Bora Ozyildiz, an employment specialist, says workers are wasting time because they're spending more hours at work and secondly, there is an inability to separate personal and professional time. But should we worry about this?

'Working life and personal life are not as separate as they once were,' Bora Ozyildiz says. The workday has grown for the American worker. 'We're talking about wasted time at work but Americans are talking about how overworked they are.' In fact socializing with co-workers was the next biggest time waster at 23%. Americans are suffering work-fatigue and time wasting helps them deal with this.

There is a change going on – the line between work-time and personal time is disappearing – work often interrupts our personal life. The workday is not just 9-to-5 any more. Employers expect people to be available outside those hours for work purposes and as a result of a lack of personal time, the things that a worker should be doing outside those work hours, things like paying bills, sometimes find their way into the office. Some 6.8% of Americans did personal business in work time. Technology makes it equally possible for them to prioritize life over work.

But not all non-productive time that an employee spends is a complete waste and maybe we should welcome this. Creative waste is an opportunity for learning. Reading an online newspaper, for example, is clearly a non-work activity for most jobs. However, the things you learn could generate a new idea for your company. That's an example of creative waste.

2

A *Will* and *going to*
B Present continuous for future plans
C Compound nouns
D **Communication strategies** Agreeing and disagreeing
E **Interaction** Five days in Dubai

Globetrotters

A *Will* and *going to*

1))) **3** Listen to a conversation on a plane. On the map, label the destination of each traveller. Label T for Turgut and H for Helen.

WORLD TRAVELLERS

• Manchester
• Zurich

• Singapore

• Sydney

2 Listen to the conversation again and complete these sentences.

1 Helen's total journey time is _____ hours.

2 She is going to meet a business partner and then have a _____ .

3 Helen _____ what she wants to see in Sydney.

4 Helen is going to go on a _____ tour.

5 She will probably go to see the _____ .

3 Label these sentences from the conversation. Use one of the options from the box.

> **a** a quick decision **b** a prediction
> **c** a plan based on evidence

1 No, I'm okay, thanks. No, actually, I will have one – I've changed my mind. ◯

2 It's about 24 hours. I'll get there at 5.15 on Sunday morning. ◯

3 I'm really going to meet our partner company ◯

4 We're going to open a joint business in the UK. ◯

5 It'll be really hot at this time of year. ◯

6 That sounds really interesting. I'll try to go there … ◯

4 Choose the correct verb to complete these sentences.

1 A passenger is shouting and fighting on the airplane. You feel the plane turning round.

The pilot *will* / *is going to* turn back and land.

2 You are invited to a party. You're not sure at first but decide to go later.

I'll / *am going to* join you later.

3 At a budgeting meeting managers cut the travel budget.

Our sales people *won't* / *are not going to* have so many trips.

4 Andrew, a colleague, is visiting so you look at the plane timetable.

The plane *will* / *is going to* arrive tomorrow afternoon.

5 Your manager is angry that you took your holiday in the middle of a busy period. I'm sorry,

I *won't* / *am not going to* do it again.

6 You are watching the Singapore Formula 1 car race. Four drivers have a chance of winning.

I'm not sure, but I think Lewis Hamilton *will* / *is going to* win.

5 Are these sentences correct (✓) or incorrect (✗)?

1 Erika has a long travel to work each day. ◯

2 You're going to go on holiday tomorrow – lucky you! Have a nice trip. ◯

3 During her year off, Aiko journeyed across Australia and New Zealand. ◯

4 They all jumped into the car and went on a journey to the coast for the day. ◯

5 The new sales manager has been to countries across Asia, Africa and South America – she's travelled a lot. ◯

6 For my holidays this year I'm going to trip to China to see the Great Wall. ◯

> ⚠ *Travel* is most often used as a verb but can also be an uncountable noun. We don't say 'a travel'.
> *Where are you **travelling** to today?* (verb)
> *Is business **travel** important for your job?* (noun)
> A **trip** is a short journey or a short period of time in a place.
> *And what is the purpose of your **trip**?*

6 Correct the sentences in exercise 5 that are wrong.

1 Read the brochure extract and the schedule below. Are these sentences true (T) or false (F)?

1 The visit is part of a twin city programme. ◯

2 Families and friends stay in each other's homes. ◯

3 The exchange programme is just for fun and a cheap holiday. ◯

4 This year, families from America are going to stay with families from Brazil. ◯

5 The families will have two organized trips. ◯

6 They are spending one day with their host families. ◯

Salvador to LA – exchange visit

Exchange your world with ours! Every year families and friends from our two twin cities stay with each other for a week. We spend time with each other's families and friends, stay in their homes, go on organized trips and have a lot of fun together. Families and friends from Los Angeles and Salvador learn more about one another and form international partnerships that help economic development, cross-cultural understanding and global cooperation. This year we're very pleased to welcome back families from Salvador and look forward to going over to Brazil again next year.

Date	Schedule	
November	a.m.	p.m.
11	Arrive at airport – meet host families and go with families to homes	Dinner with mayor of Los Angeles – all
12	Trip to California Science Center	Hollywood bus tour
13	Free day with host family	
14	Trip to Malibu	Dinner at Paradise Cove Beach café
15	Free day with host family	
16	Farewell lunch – all	Plane departs for Salvador

2 Look at the schedule again and complete the email. Use the present continuous or *will* with the verbs in brackets.

Dear Madalena,

We're so pleased you ¹_____ (stay) with us for the sister city exchange program. We hope you ²_____ (like) Los Angeles – we've planned a lot of interesting things to do and places to see. Some of these ³_____ (be) with the official sister city exchange program but on the other days we're taking you along with us. We are going with you to the Science Center on the second day but we aren't going on the bus tour. On the third day of the trip we're taking you to Griffin Park. We ⁴_____ (ride) horses there and there's a nice place to have lunch at Crystal Springs, so we are having a picnic outside on the 13th. You're going on a trip to the beach at Malibu and we ⁵_____ (meet) you all later at the Paradise Cove café. On the 15th we're spending the day at Disneyland® Park at Anaheim. We ⁶_____ (visit) the Indiana Jones Adventure in the afternoon and at night we will watch the firework display – we hope it ⁷_____ (be) a day for you to remember.

So that's the schedule for your visit – let us know if there's anything else you want to see or do. Let us know about any preferences you have for food and we ⁸_____ (get) it for you.

See you soon,

Bonnie

3 Put the words in brackets in order. Complete the questions.

1 Are you booking the hotel? (book/will/you) an en-suite room for us? _Will you book_

2 (leaving/the/is/bus/tour) at one or two in the afternoon? _____

3 (help/you/will/me) to close the cases? I've packed most things. _____

4 We're going on the college trip to the cinema on Thursday – (too/you/are/coming) ? _____

5 We're quite late to get a cheap flight to Italy. (cost/how/much/it/will/now) ? _____

6 (are/you/where/going) on your holiday? _____

1 Look at the hotel review below and tick (✓) the facilities *CitizenM* hotels offer.

1 reception ⬭
2 flat screen TV ⬭
3 pool ⬭
4 gym ⬭
5 food centre ⬭
6 movies ⬭
7 WiFi ⬭
8 concierge ⬭
9 business centre ⬭
10 executive suite ⬭

2 Read the hotel review again and choose the correct answers.

1 The hotel rooms are all (*the same/different/a bit different*).

2 The hotel's aim is to provide (*luxury accommodation/cheap accommodation/good value rooms*).

3 The toilet is (*outside/in the room/in the hall*).

4 One of the room's walls is a (*cinema screen/window/bookshelf*).

5 Guests can change the (*lighting and music/music and heating/TV*).

6 The writer (*likes/dislikes/hates*) the hotel.

3 Complete the compound nouns. Use words from the review.

1 five-_____ hotel
2 _____ shower
3 king-_____ bed
4 _____ service
5 honey _____
6 _____ top
7 flat_____ TV
8 _____ centre

4 Complete the conversation. Use the compound nouns from exercise 3.

Liza: Congratulations on your wedding! How was your [1]_____?

Agnes: It was great – our hotel was terrific! We watched films on a [2]_____ built into the wall, from our [3]_____ bed.

Liza: So how many stars was the hotel?

Agnes: It was a [4]_____ hotel – right in the middle of the countryside.

Liza: And what was the service like?

Agnes: Well, everyone was very kind and if you ordered anything from your room the [5]_____ was very quick. It had great facilities – WiFi, on-demand films, a [6]_____ shower and swimming pool . . .

Liza: That sounds wonderful!

Agnes: But the main problem was my new husband – he kept going into the hotel [7]_____ to check his work emails on his [8]_____ computer – so annoying!

CITIZEN hotels

Even from the outside there seems to be something a bit different about the CitizenM hotel. As you get nearer it looks like individually made concrete blocks all put on top of each other. And that's exactly what it is: individual rooms offering the same hotel experience no matter where you go or which CitizenM hotel you go to.

CitizenM hotels offer affordable luxury – a five-star designer hotel at budget prices and it's the pre-made rooms that allow them to do this. The next thing you'll notice is there is no check-in, reception, room service or concierge. At CitizenM you will be greeted in the lobby by a helper, who will assist you through the electronic check-in process.

Every room is just 14 square metres – just enough for one or two people but no more. In order to save space, and to make the room itself seem bigger,

CitizenM placed the walk-in power shower and toilet in individual tubes inside the room. The shower tube is transparent and the toilet tube isn't. The window is large, taking up the entire back of the room and in front of the window is the king-size bed. Each room is the same so you won't find any executive or honeymoon suites but you can change the room to your individual mood. The room experience is centred around the mood pad, something like a palmtop that lets you select or create different room environments by changing the music and lighting. There is no gym or pool but CitizenM offers plenty of other modern facilities like free WiFi to all its guests and free movies in the room on a flatscreen TV.

Most of the bottom floor of the hotel is a common space with a food centre, a small business centre and several more areas for socializing. This new concept in hotels is fashionable and at €69 a night, very affordable.

1 Read the article opposite. Which countries are the most and least friendly for Americans, according to the writer?

2 ⟩⟩ **4** Listen to a discussion about the survey. Decide who holds each opinion: Nirav (N), Adèle (A) or Mary (M).

1 The survey is silly. (A)

2 The article has some good points. ◯

3 It's easy to make friends when you speak the language. ◯

4 The differences in culture make it difficult to make friends. ◯

5 People don't try hard enough to integrate. ◯

6 People don't want to make friends with someone who will leave soon. ◯

3 Listen again and complete these sentences.

1 _____ , I don't agree – I thought it was quite interesting.

2 Me too. It had a _____ about Americans …

3 I _____ that's true at all – it's easy to make friends …

4 _____ Adèle but there are other reasons for this too – …

5 _____ but many people do make friends in spite of cultural differences

6 _____ , Mary?

7 _____ – it's the people who go to the other country who don't try …

8 But _____ there is a more important point?

9 I'm _____ , but the article is very general.

10 _____ , that's what I mean …

4 Complete the table with these phrases.

> Actually, I think you're wrong there.   I think so.   Uhuh.
> ~~Sure.~~   I'll have to think about that.   Sorry but I don't agree.
> Yes, but …   No way!   Maybe.   You've got a good point.

	Informal	Formal
Agreeing	*Sure*	
Uncertain		
Disagreeing		

The world's friendliest countries

America used to have everything – good jobs, a booming economy, and plenty of housing, but when the economy goes down people leave to go abroad. HSBC Bank surveyed 2,155 people living in other countries. They gave their new country points according to ability to make friends with local people, joining a community group, learning the language and buying property. According to the survey, Canada is the most welcoming; almost 95% said they have made friends with locals. In Germany, 92% made local friends and in Australia 91% found local friends. Americans gave China, India and United Arab Emirates low scores because cultural differences made integration difficult. ∎

5 Read these sentences and find three incorrect sentences. The first one has been done for you.

1 **a** You know, British people never say what they think, don't you agree?
  b ⟨I agree you – they are so polite.⟩

2 **a** It's very cold in here, isn't it?
  b I don't think so.

3 **a** Henri doesn't like his meal. He says it's too salty.
  b I think that too – there's too much salt. I can't taste the food.

4 **a** Marcus is difficult to talk to – he's so aggressive.
  b Yes, I agree so – it's not easy to give your own opinion.

> ⚠ *Agree* and *disagree* are verbs so we use *do* to form questions and negatives.
> I **don't agree**.   **Does** anyone **agree** with me?

6   Correct the sentences from exercise 5 that are wrong.

1 Read the leaflet, *Tours Around Dubai* and match the tours with A–D on the map.

2 Read these profiles of three people attending a conference in Dubai. Decide which tour each person would enjoy.

Property development conference, Dubai

Participants

Derek Jones _____
likes: museums, culture, history
dislikes: shopping, cities

Aylin Karabulat _____
likes: shopping, entertainment, city life
dislikes: museums, countryside

Francesca Musci _____
likes: being active, nature, camping
dislikes: sitting around, museums, shopping

---

3 Find ten words from the leaflet in the wordsearch. The first one has been done for you.

B	J	V	O	B	T	B	L	L	H	U	W	S	W	Y
A	F	Q	Q	G	X	C	Z	O	F	I	D	A	B	K
R	K	P	Q	O	A	S	I	S	A	H	S	N	E	K
B	C	A	M	P	S	I	T	E	J	Z	S	D	L	X
E	W	W	A	R	W	G	S	K	H	D	G	B	L	O
C	B	J	R	P	R	E	O	T	K	H	P	O	Y	D
U	C	L	X	O	H	N	U	Z	T	O	Z	A	D	E
E	R	I	Y	E	Y	Z	K	C	V	W	V	R	A	S
S	D	U	N	E	B	A	S	H	I	N	G	D	N	M
Q	I	T	G	S	I	S	N	W	J	V	N	I	C	T
C	H	H	G	N	C	Q	I	L	S	L	U	N	I	M
H	J	U	J	K	E	Q	F	T	Q	I	T	G	N	M
A	R	C	H	I	T	E	C	T	U	R	E	L	G	F
E	O	E	H	Y	T	I	Q	K	P	U	D	G	F	S
L	E	I	S	U	R	E	F	A	C	I	L	I	T	Y

TOURS AROUND **DUBAI**

1 Sharjah, one of the cultural centres of the Middle East, is only 20 minutes north of Dubai. Anyone with an interest in history, culture and architecture will enjoy exploring this old coastal city. Our tour starts at the old city, where the buildings in the Heritage Centre, formerly the homes of wealthy families, are now museums showing Arabian lifestyle 200 years ago. We go on to the Natural History Museum, and end at the fabulous Souq Al Arsah, Sharjah's oldest market, where the city's real history lies amongst the narrow streets with their typical Arabic architecture and hundreds of shops.

2 The East Coast tour takes you around a variety of landscapes and activities within the Emirates. It includes a desert where you can go sand boarding or dune bashing, the mountains and the sea. There are a number of stops including Masafi, in the mountains, and Diba Al Hisn, a local fishing town where you can visit the harbour in the evening to see the day's catch and to buy fish for a campsite barbecue.

3 Al Ain is known as the 'Garden City' and is 1.5 hours' drive from Dubai. The city is a large oasis in the desert. We go to the beautiful Buraimi Oasis and then onto the Buraimi souk, the Al Ain Museum, and the camel souk as well as some of the spectacular palaces. We will stay overnight in the desert and there will be an opportunity to go dune bashing the next morning.

4 South west of Dubai is Abu Dhabi – the capital of the United Arab Emirates and one of the most wealthy and rapidly developing cities in the world. It's a cosmopolitan city rising out of the desert with luxury hotels, shopping malls, entertainment and leisure facilities. The city also has many parks and tree-lined streets. Some of its history as a fishing village still remains and the tour includes the beautiful coast, the dhow-building yards and visits to a number of palaces.

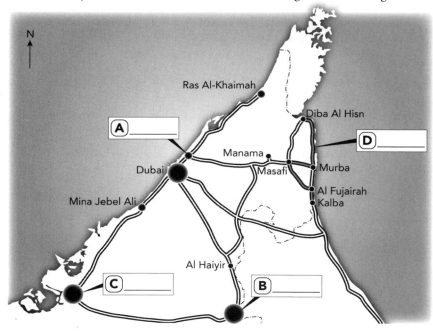

3

Be my guest

Chez Georges

A Base form with *to* or *-ing* form

1 Read this article and look at the pictures. Tick (✓) the things you should do and cross (✗) the things you shouldn't do.

Dining etiquette in France

Differences in the way cultures eat are a good conversation starter and the French love good conversation. However, there are some things to watch out for . . .

¹_____ salt and pepper to a meal before ²_____ it will make most French chefs very angry. It is considered to be unacceptable ³_____ for ketchup. They believe it hides the taste of the meal. While eating in France, it is always polite to have both of your hands in view over the table. Also when ⁴_____ at night in a restaurant, you should ⁵_____ your mobile phone. The French make a clear distinction between work and leisure and if your phone rings, people may ⁶_____ at you.

If you pause during the meal, it is usual to show that you intend ⁷_____ some more by putting your knife and fork on each side of the plate, but still on the plate. When you've finished eating, put them on the plate together in the middle.

When you are ready to leave, the best way ⁸_____ the bill is to catch the attention of the waiter or waitress by 'writing' in the air with one hand.

2 Read the text again and complete it. Use the infinitive with *to*, the infinitive without *to* or the *-ing* form of the verbs in the box.

> stare taste add eat (x 2) ask
> switch off request

3 Read the conversations and complete the sentences. Use the infinitive form with *to* or the *-ing* form of verbs. In some sentences both forms are correct.

1
Marietta: Let's have dinner later.
Charles: Oh, but I'm hungry now.
Marietta didn't want to delay *having* dinner.

2
Marietta: I'd rather not eat late. It's really bad for the digestion.
Charles: Let's go now then.
_____ late is really bad, according to Marietta.

3
Marietta: Don't wait for me – your food is getting cold.
Charles: Well, if you're sure.
Marietta wanted Charles to start _____ .

4
Marietta: Charles, could you pass the salt, please?
Charles: Of course.
Marietta asked Charles _____ the salt.

5
Marietta: That was a nice meal. Shall we ask for the bill?
Charles: Yes, let's pay. It's time to go.
Charles thought it was time _____ .

6
Marietta: Shall we leave the waiter a tip?
Charles: Yes, we should. He's been very good.
Marietta wanted _____ a tip.

7
Marietta: That was a lovely meal. It's so nice to have a good restaurant close to home.
Charles: Yes, it is.
Marietta and Charles liked _____ a good restaurant near home.

1 🔊 **5** Listen to Yi Wen and Marina having a business lunch and tick (✓) the correct answers.

1 They are going to have food from …
a Malta ◯
b Malaysia ◯
c Morocco ◯

2 Yi Wen recommends …
a fish soup ◯
b fried fish ◯
c fish curry ◯

3 They eat the food with …
a bread ◯
b noodles ◯
c rice ◯

2 Listen again and answer the questions.

1 What are they going to talk about over lunch? _____
2 Why does Yi Wen recommend the fish? _____
3 What can't Marina eat it? _____
4 How do they eat it? _____

3 Complete these sentences from the conversation in exercises 1 and 2. Use the phrases in this box.

> must try   like   would you like   sounds good
> does it taste   for inviting me   help yourself
> is there anything   what's in   recommend
> come with   can't really eat

1 Oh, it's lovely here – what a nice restaurant. Thanks _____ .
2 Now, what _____ ?
3 Yes, please help. What would you _____ ?
4 You _____ the fish head curry.
5 Fish head curry – what's that _____ ?
6 What _____ like?
7 Oh, I _____ food that's too spicy.
8 And _____ it?
9 That _____ . I'll go with that.
10 The waiter will put the curry in the middle of the table and you _____ to the food.
11 OK. What does it _____ ? Do you eat it with bread?
12 Now for the next course – _____ you don't eat?

4 Match the correct combinations. Use a good dictionary to help you.

1 raw / scrambled / fried / hard-boiled   a steak
2 olive / almond / corn / sunflower   b fish
3 hot / chilli / mild / vegetable   c fruit
4 fillet / sirloin / T-bone / rump   d curry
5 white / grilled / baked / fried   e egg
6 tinned / dried / fresh / soft   f oil

5 Choose the correct word to complete the sentences.

1 A: How would you like your steak, madam?
   B: I'll have it *tender / rare / cooked / grilled*, please.

2 A: What would you like to drink?
   B: I'll just have water please – *soft / white / sparkling / homemade* water.

3 A: Which kind of vegetables come with the meal?
   B: We have mixed *stewed / bottled / steamed / low-fat* broccoli and carrots.

4 For dessert we have *strawberry / roasted / still / egg* ice cream.

6 Complete the sentences. Use the words in the box.

> chewy   salty   spicy   delicious   rich

1 How much chilli did you put in here? The curry is so _____ it's burning my mouth!
2 Quick, give me a drink of water – that food is too _____ .
3 Could I have some more dessert? It's really _____ .
4 This steak is really tough to eat. It's very _____ – it's going to take all day to eat it.
5 I'm sorry, I can't eat another thing. The food is lovely but it's very _____ and filling.

1 Look at the article below and match the food with the things they help.

1 apples   **a** poor vision

2 tea   **b** weight control

3 broccoli   **c** bones

4 olive oil   **d** skin and gums

5 bread   **e** cholesterol levels

2 Read the article and put the quantifiers (in bold) into this table.

negatives and questions	countable	*many*
	uncountable	1 _____
small quantities	countable	*a few*
	uncountable	2 _____
more than something we need or want	countable	*too many*
	uncountable	3 _____
large amounts	noun	4 _____
	no noun	*a lot (of)*
the right amount or less than we need or want	countable	*(not) enough*
	uncountable	

3 Complete these questions with *many* or *much*.

1 How _____ kinds of apple are there?

2 How _____ broccoli do we need to eat every day?

3 How _____ olive oil should we use?

4 How _____ calories does a tablespoon of olive oil contain?

5 How _____ salt did bread contain in the past?

4 Read the article again and answer the questions in exercise 3.

5 Choose the correct word or phrase to complete these conversations.

A: Is there ¹*any / a little / many* sugar in this coffee?

B: Yes, I put three spoonfuls in it.

A: Oh no, that's ²*too much / too few / too enough* for me.

A: How much food have you made for the after-conference party tonight?

B: I've made ³*enough / too much / a little* for four people.

A: That's ⁴*too much / too few / not enough* – another two people are coming.

A: Could I have ⁵*a few / a little / many* more potatoes, please?

B: I'm sorry, there aren't ⁶*any / no / much* more – I didn't make enough.

Superfoods

Superfoods are foods which are full of vitamins and minerals and are especially good for your health. Here are some of the best.

Apples
How many different kinds of apples are there? **A lot** – over 7000, in fact, and they are full of vitamin C for healthy skin and gums – just one apple is **enough** to give you a quarter of your daily vitamin C.

Tea
Tea comes in **many** different forms – black, green, or white. All of these may prevent your bones from becoming weaker and may help them to stay healthy as you age. People who drink two or more cups of green or black tea per day have been found to have good bone strength.

Broccoli
Just **a little** broccoli is enough each day – two pieces should be enough. Broccoli contains vitamin C and could help fight poor eyesight and going blind when you are older.

Olive oil
A few studies suggest that the fat in olive oil is good for your heart – it decreases cholesterol levels. Olive oil is one of the main ingredients in the healthy Mediterranean diet. A little is enough – **too much** can be fattening. A tablespoon of olive oil contains **lots of** calories – as **many** as a large slice of bread and butter.

Wholegrain bread
Bread with a **lot of** seeds could protect you against heart disease and help to keep your weight under control by stopping you from feeling hungry. In the past, bread contained a lot of salt. However, manufacturers don't use **much** salt in their bread nowadays.

1))) **6** Listen to the telephone conversation and put these sentences in order.

Kasia makes an excuse.	☐
Susie asks Kasia about her plans.	①️
Kasia says *No* again.	☐
They arrange to meet another time.	☐
Susie invites Kasia to go bowling.	②️
Susie gives Kasia a reason to take a break from work.	☐
Kasia asks about Susie's friend.	☐

2 Listen again and complete this conversation with the phrases in the box.

> I won't insist   do you want to join us   I understand
> I'd love to   I don't think I can   if you insist

Susie: A group of us are going bowling at the Super Bowl –
¹_____ ?

Kasia: Oh, ²_____ . I really like bowling but I'm sorry I can't go. I'm giving a presentation the next day.

Kasia: It sounds like good fun but ³_____ .

Susie: Oh, OK, Kasia. ⁴_____ but it's a pity.

Susie: It's OK, ⁵_____ . You don't have to come.

Kasia: All right, you can bring him, ⁶_____ !

3 Put the expressions in this box under the correct heading in the table below.

> Perhaps we could meet again another time?   Er
> Thank you for thinking of me   I really like bowling
> I'm sorry, I can't go   It sounds like good fun but
> Let's arrange another time   thanks for inviting me anyway
> I'm really sorry but   Oh

Hesitate	Apologize	Suggest an alternative	Say something positive	Say thank you

4 Match each offer with the most appropriate refusal.

1 How about a game of tennis this weekend?   a No, thanks – I'm on a diet.

2 Do you want some coffee?   b No, I've got to wash my hair.

3 Would you like some chocolate cake?   c I can't, I'm allergic to seafood.

4 Would you like to come to the cinema tonight?   d I'm sorry, I've hurt my arm.

5 Do try the lobster, it's delicious.   e No, my feet are killing me.

6 Would you like to dance?   f No, thanks, it keeps me awake.

1 Read the article opposite. Tick (✓) the things that are acceptable and cross (✗) the things that are not acceptable.

1 giving gifts in private ◯

2 giving your gift with two hands ◯

3 opening the gift later ◯

4 giving valuable presents in front of other people ◯

5 taking a photo of the gift ◯

6 giving a gift during business negotiations ◯

7 wrapping the gift in red ◯

8 giving four of one thing ◯

2 Look at the article again and answer these questions.

1 Why may a business gift not be accepted? _____

2 Why will a gift be refused three times? _____

3 Why are gifts opened in private? _____

4 Why is it bad to give four of the same thing? _____

3 Read the definitions and find words in the article to complete this crossword. Then find an expression meaning *good luck*.

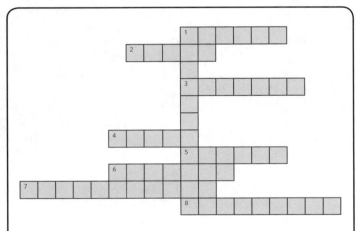

1 Always wanting more food, money, power or possessions.

2 A custom that says you must avoid an activity or subject either because it is offensive or because it is against your religion.

3 To say 'no' politely.

4 To end a relationship with someone, especially because of a disagreement.

5 Difficult to deal with because it is complicated and full of problems.

6 Something that you say or do to show how you feel about someone.

7 Spending or costing a lot of money.

8 To make someone feel ashamed, nervous or uncomfortable, especially in front of other people

Giving gifts in China

GIFT-GIVING IN CHINA HAS TRADITIONALLY BEEN A very important part of the culture. For the outsider, understanding what to give and how can be tricky and this is complicated by the fact that giving gifts in business is not allowed today.

However, in many organizations, attitudes towards gifts are beginning to relax but when people give gifts to individuals, they do it in private and say that it is a gift for friendship, not for business. The Chinese will usually decline a gift three times before finally accepting, so that they do not appear greedy. Each time a gift is refused, the giver continues to offer it and when it has been taken, they tell the person they're happy the gift has been accepted. Gifts are offered with both hands and are always wrapped. The gift is put to one side and opened later – this tradition is so that the other person will not show any disappointment with the gift in front of the giver.

Valuable gifts are never given to one person in front of other people because this can cause embarrassment (especially with the rule against gift-giving in business) – and gifts should not be too extravagant. Photographs of any gift-giving are not taken unless the gift is being presented to an organization.

Giving a gift to the whole company, rather than an individual, can be acceptable in Chinese business culture but all business negotiations should be completed before gifts are exchanged. The gift is given to the leader of the Chinese team and often with an explanation of the meaning of the gift.

Red is a lucky colour and gifts are often wrapped in this colour. Pink, gold and silver are also acceptable colours for wrapping paper. Eight is considered one of the luckiest numbers in Chinese culture. If you receive eight of any item, it is a gesture of good will. Six is good fortune but four of any item is taboo because the Cantonese word for *four* sounds similar to *death*. Other gifts to avoid are scissors or knives as this means you would like to cut or sever the relationship.

4

A *can, could* and *be able to*
B Personal characteristics
C Comparatives and superlatives
D **Communication strategies** Building on ideas
E **Interaction** Training solutions

Learning curve

A Can, could and be able to

1 Read the article below and write *AJ*, *EP* or *both* next to the sentences.

1 _____ can remember their most recent thoughts.

2 _____ can remember nearly everyday of her life.

3 _____ has two kinds of memory loss.

2 Look at the article again and complete these sentences with *can('t)*, or *is(n't)* / *was(n't) able to*. Some questions have more than one possible answer.

1 AJ _____ stop her memories.

2 AJ _____ remember the time and date of phone calls.

3 AJ can remember difficult things she _____ do.

4 EP _____ remember things after 1960.

5 We _____ to partly understand what life is like for AJ and EP.

3 Complete these sentences with *can(n't)*, *could(n't)* or a form of *be able to*. Some questions have more than one possible answer.

1 Although Gary Kasparov _____ beat almost everyone at chess, he _____ beat the computer *Deep Blue*.

2 Stefano started the crossword puzzle yesterday but he _____ finish it .

3 Being _____ think about a subject from a different point of view is called *lateral thinking*.

4 Kim Peek (on whom the main character in the film *Rain Man* was based) _____ recall the content of 12,000 books. However, he _____ do complicated maths problems.

5 Despite all the disadvantages, our team _____ win the contract.

6 When I was young I _____ speak German but I haven't been there for years and I _____ communicate in German any more.

Remember this

There is a 41-year-old woman, an administrative assistant from California called 'AJ', who remembers almost every day of her life since age 11. There is an 85-year-old man, a retired lab technician called 'EP', who remembers only his most recent thought. She might have the best memory in the world. He could have the worst.

'My memory flows like a movie-nonstop and is uncontrollable,' says AJ. She can remember that at 12.34 p.m. on Sunday, 3 August, 1986, a young man she liked called her on the telephone. She can remember that on 28 March, 1992, she had lunch with her father at the Beverly Hills Hotel. She can remember world events and trips to the store, the weather, difficult tasks she was able to do and how she felt at that time. Almost every day is there.

EP has two types of memory loss – the first means he can't form new memories and the second means he can't remember old memories either, at least not since 1960. His childhood, World War II – all that is perfectly clear. But as far as he knows, gas costs less than a dollar a gallon and the moon landing never happened.

AJ and EP are extremes of human memory. Though the rest of us are somewhere between these extremes of remembering everything and remembering nothing, we're all able to partly understand the incredible memory of AJ and the terrible fate of EP.

1 Read the job adverts opposite and complete them with the words in the box.

> of problem for pressure able attention

2 Look at the adverts again and find words which mean the following.

1 able to use a computer _____

2 thinking about things in a detailed and intelligent way so that you can examine and understand things _____

3 careful to do everything it is your job or duty to do _____

4 sure that you can do things well _____

5 good at finding ways of dealing with practical problems _____

6 using a thinking process in which facts and ideas are connected in a correct way _____

3 Match these questions with the answers below. Some questions have more than one possible answer.

1 What is your biggest weakness? _____

2 What are your best skills? _____

3 Can you describe your personality? _____

4 Do you prefer to work by yourself or with others? _____

a I'm a good team player.

b I've got a good sense of humour.

c I'm good at thinking on my feet.

d I've got an outgoing personality.

e I like to work on my own initiative.

f I can be a bit too bossy.

4 Is each sentence correct (✓) or incorrect (✗)?

1 Keiko has got a very good work – she's a designer. ◯

2 What kind of work does she do? ◯

3 She usually designs books but she also works on a lot of other things. ◯

4 That sounds like a nice work – creative. ◯

5 Yes, she trained to be a designer after she lost her last work in her old company. ◯

> ⚠ *Job* is generally a noun:
> *What's your **job**? I'm a software engineer. Have you finished all those **jobs**? Work* can be a verb or a noun.
> *She **works** for a software company. We start **work** at 8 a.m.*
> Notice that *work* is an uncountable noun, so it cannot be plural.
> *Have you finished all that **work**?* NOT ~~Have you finished all those works.~~

5 Correct the sentences in exercise 4 that are wrong.

6 Look at this wordsearch. Find ten adjectives to describe characteristics.

New South Wales Office of Fair Trading

We are an ambitious organization responsible
1 _____ consumer policy and are currently looking for two people.

JOB TITLE:
Strategy Director
SALARY: $65–80k

Central Canberra

About the role: You will provide strategic insight that enables the Office of Fair Trading to provide leadership in competition and consumer policy.

About you: You should be capable 2 _____ strategic thinking, have self-confidence, be resourceful and conscientious and be able to work well under 3 _____.

JOB TITLE:
Economic Adviser
SALARY: Up to $57k

Central Canberra

About the role: You will provide economic analysis to projects that are of major importance to the economy. You need to be 4 _____ to analyse the main issues of the projects and develop logical solutions to problems.

About you: You will have excellent analytical skills, good 5 _____ to detail with practical experience in markets analysis, be computer literate and have good 6 _____-solving skills.

U	B	R	E	S	C	E	U	T	A	L	R	M	R	F
F	U	E	T	E	M	O	T	I	V	A	T	E	D	M
E	S	L	E	R	F	E	R	V	I	N	V	A	U	P
F	N	I	N	X	U	I	I	E	L	E	L	E	E	P
F	U	A	E	S	U	V	F	E	F	U	E	O	T	I
I	R	B	E	L	F	S	T	L	U	T	F	L	S	U
C	T	L	V	A	U	T	B	T	E	E	U	E	E	E
I	S	E	L	F	S	U	F	F	I	C	I	E	N	T
E	N	U	N	P	U	N	C	T	U	A	L	B	S	E
N	V	S	M	N	F	A	F	E	T	T	L	F	I	B
T	R	E	S	O	U	R	C	E	F	U	L	P	B	L
U	E	F	L	E	X	I	B	L	E	S	L	E	L	U
P	E	R	S	U	A	S	I	V	E	R	M	S	E	T
L	E	U	S	N	U	M	E	R	A	T	E	F	C	S

1 Put the words in the box into the groups a–e below.

> one-to-one professor in-service intensive online
> part-time PhD lecturer self-study diploma

a qualifications   _____, _____

b training   _____, _____

c distance learning   _____, _____

d course period   _____, _____

e teachers   _____, _____

2 Look at the article below and find the following.

a two words related to teaching methods _online_ , _____

b two words for *teacher* _____, _____

c two words about course length _____, _____

3 Look at the article again. Are these sentences true (T) or false (F)?

1 Electric City is a software company. ◯

2 e-leaning improved company profits. ◯

3 Staff took just over 2 million e-lessons. ◯

4 Employees stay with the company longer because of e-learning. ◯

4 Complete this table. Use the correct form of words from the article.

Adjective	Comparative	Adverb	Superlative
quick	quicker	1 _____	quickest
low	2 _____	low	lowest
short	shorter	shortly	3 _____
good	4 _____	well	best
fast	5 _____	fast	fastest
popular	more popular	popularly	6 _____
great	7 _____	greatly	greatest
rapid	more rapid	8 _____	most rapid

5 Complete the sentences with the comparative or superlative.

1 Online learning is _more flexible_ (flexible) than traditional classroom learning.

2 Students find that learning in their own time is _____ (relax) than learning in college.

3 Electronic products are developing much _____ (quick) than staff can be trained to sell them.

4 It is _____ (cheap) to learn part time than it is to take a full-time course.

5 Training staff is one of the _____ (important) parts of company activity.

6 *New Horizons* is the world's _____ (big) IT training company.

e-learning for profit

Electric City, an electronics retailer, sells products that are rapidly changing and improving. The company found that the key to increasing profits is an expert sales staff, so they needed a way of teaching 45,000 sales staff more quickly to become experts in their sales area.

With electronic products, shelf-lives* are shorter than other products and on-the-job staff training is a continual process. This led the company to replace its extensive classroom training process with web-based online learning programs. Since the program began, *Electric City's* employees have taken more than one million e-classes with the result that they have gained better knowledge and skills in half the time and at a lower cost than traditional classroom-based training*.

As we move rapidly to a business culture where learning equals earning, more efficient employee training means faster sales. Traditional classroom methods can be too slow for training staff in new products and services, which are coming out more and more rapidly. While full-time classroom training with an instructor is still important, blended e-learning, which combines classroom learning with a trainer and e-learning, is becoming the most popular form of learning.

Since the programme began three years ago, training costs and time spent in training have gone down by a third and recruitment costs are also down because staff stay with the company longer. e-learning makes staff training a more central company activity that results in greater profits and better sales staff.

shelf-life = the amount of time a product has in a store before it needs to be replaced

classroom-based training = training in a classroom with a teacher

1 Read the article below and tick (✓) the skills and activities involved in improvising.

1 listening skills ⬭ 5 respecting colleagues ⬭
2 negotiation skills ⬭ 6 sales techniques ⬭
3 presentation skills ⬭ 7 brainstorming ⬭
4 organizational skills ⬭ 8 team building ⬭

2))) 7 Listen to the conversation and complete Angela's notes for Luca.

Talk to Luca about
Marketing Manager's visit

1 Meeting room isn't _____ .

2 Suggest using _____ room.

3 Checked _____ area is available but it's being used.

4 Suggest big room in local _____ .

5 Check availability of _____ director.

The Applied Improvisation Co.

What is business improvisation?

Business improvisation is the ability to think clearly and to access creativity in the moment and under pressure in order to solve problems. It is the process followed to achieve objectives despite unexpected events. Basic techniques such as 'Yes …, and …' and more complex techniques relating to how we think, listening skills, and brainstorming are used. Improvisation is especially good in activities within business such as presentation skills and organizing events. It can be something like simple team-building skills to more complex skills such as presentation skills and brainstorming. Participants in 'improv' (improvisation) workshops learn a new way of thinking: a new respect for others, how to be 'in the moment', how to make positive choices that keep doors open, proactive listening as opposed to passive listening, trusting one another to do the right thing and the benefits of watching your colleague's back.

What we do

At the Applied Improvisation Co. we train your employees to …

3 Listen to the conversation again and complete the sentences.

1 I was actually thinking of another room. _____ one of the computer rooms.

2 _____ have an informal meeting there?

3 _____ booking the restaurant over the street?

4 _____ and _____ tell her that's what we planned all along?

5 _____ . And we could ask the managing director to come too.

4 Put the phrases in this box into the correct column below.

> I'll go along with that. Great idea. Let's…
> It might be a good idea to… Could we…?
> Why don't we…? Sounds good to me. Yes and…

Making suggestions	Agreeing with and building on ideas

5 Put the parts of the sentences in the correct order.

1 It (be/an/might/if/idea) you help Jan with the office move. _____

2 Yes, (if/about/what/and) I help him with his filing system too. _____

3 (to/good/sounds/me). Why don't you ask him if that's OK? _____

4 Yes, (go/will/along/I/with) that. I'll ask him right away. _____

1 Match the words 1–3 with the definitions a–c.

1 aggressive

2 assertive

3 passive

a behaving in a confident way, so that people notice you _____

b behaving in an angry threatening way, as if you want to fight or attack someone _____

c accepting things that happen to you or things that people say to you, without taking any action _____

2 Read the assertiveness training checklist below and follow the instructions.

3 How assertive are you? Check your score in the answer key.

4 Complete these definitions with the words from the box. You may need to change the form of the word.

| consider adapt assist improve mediate deal with |

1 When we _____ , we to try to end a quarrel between two people, groups or countries.

2 To _____ is to make something better, or to become better.

3 To _____ is to help someone to do something.

4 Someone who _____ gradually changes their behaviour and attitudes in order to be successful in a new situation.

5 To take the necessary action in order to solve a problem is to _____ something.

6 To _____ something is to think about something carefully, especially before making a choice or decision.

Assertiveness checklist

Before your assertiveness training course, we'd like to find out how assertive you actually are. Please complete the training checklist and bring it with you to the first session. The questionnaire is in two parts.

For questions 1–10, write:

1 if you rarely do this

2 if you sometimes do this

3 if you often do this

A Doing things by myself

1 I don't usually need anyone to assist me. ☐

2 I find it easy to adapt to new situations. ☐

3 I like starting conversations with people I don't know. ☐

B Protecting myself

4 I find it easy to say 'no'. ☐

5 I know my limits and I don't try to do too much. ☐

C Making positive comments

6 I find it easy to make positive comments to people. ☐

7 I tell people that I care about them. ☐

8 If I consider that someone has done a good job, I tell them. ☐

D Saying negative things

9 If I buy a something which is faulty, I feel confident about returning it. ☐

10 I don't have a problem disagreeing with someone. ☐

For questions 11–20, write:

1 if you often do this.

2 if you sometimes do this.

3 if you rarely do this

A Doing things by myself

11 I spend a lot of time on my own. ☐

12 I don't easily make new friends. ☐

B Protecting myself

13 I usually do what people tell me to do. ☐

14 I do some things because someone asked me to, not because I want to. ☐

15 If I'm invited out socially I often make an excuse not to go. ☐

C Giving positive comments

16 I find it difficult to be positive about myself. ☐

17 I'm quite negative towards others sometimes. ☐

D Saying negative things

18 I find it difficult to deal with problems face to face. ☐

19 If I'm unhappy, I try to smile so that I don't have to talk about it. ☐

20 I find it difficult to mediate in an argument. ☐

A Present perfect and past simple
B *used to*
C Conversation topics
D **Communication Strategies** Socializing
E **Interaction** Choosing a candidate

Getting on

A Present perfect and past simple

1 Read the article, 'You're Fired!'. In what order do you read about the objects shown in the pictures? Label the photographs 1–3.

2 Read the article again and answer true (T) or false (F).

1 His father made clothes. ⬭

2 His company increased in value in the 1980s. ⬭

3 Alan Sugar has been running a football team since the 1990s. ⬭

4 He decided to go into telecommunications in the 1990s. ⬭

5 *The Apprentice* has been a great success. ⬭

3 Write complete sentences about Lord Sugar's experiences.

1 (sold/TV aerials/the past) *He sold TV aerials in the past.*

2 (own/consumer electronics company since 1968) _____

3 (bought Betacom and Viglen/1990s) _____

4 (sold/shares/football club/1994) _____

5 (since 2005 / star / a television show) _____

4 Complete the article below. Choose the correct form of the verb.

One of the finest football players today [1]*is / has been* Cristiano Ronaldo. He [2]*has been / was* born in 1985 in Portugal and [3]*has developed / developed* his love for football at the age of three. At the age of eleven he [4]*has joined / joined* Sporting Lisbon. Since then he [5]*played / has played* for Manchester United and Real Madrid. Ronaldo [6]*has also done / also did* some charity work. In 2005, he [7]*has helped / helped* victims of the Tsunami disaster in Indonesia and raised £66,000 pounds by selling some of his sports gear. Recently he [8]*worked / has worked* with the Red Cross to raise money for landmine victims in Afghanistan.

YOU'RE FIRED!

Alan Michael Sugar was born on 24 March 1947, the son of a tailor. After he left school he went into business selling products such as TV aerials. He then founded Amstrad in 1968 and the company moved into consumer electronics. In 1980 Amstrad was listed on the London Stock Exchange and the company doubled in both profit and market value every year throughout the 1980s. In 1984, Amstrad started producing computers. Alan Sugar then purchased the controlling interest* in a London football club. Unfortunately, this wasn't a successful business venture and he sold his shares ten years later. In the 1990s, Amstrad bought into Betacom and Viglen, to focus more on telecommunications. In 2000, Amstrad released its combined telephone and e-mail device, called the e-m@iler. Alan Sugar now stars in the successful TV series 'The Apprentice', which has had several series since 2005. In the series, Lord Sugar gives job candidates things to do such as creating an advertising campaign for a product or taking part in a job interview. At the end of each show he tells one person to leave, saying 'You're fired!' and at the end of the series he tells the one remaining candidate 'You're hired!' Since then Lord Sugar has written a book about the show called *The Apprentice – How to get hired, not fired*.

controlling interest = when you own enough shares to be able to make decisions about what happens to the company

1 Read this article and complete the information about Miranda and her father.

Career chart

Miranda's father ⟶ navy ⟶ 1_____
Miranda ⟶ 2_____ ⟶ civil service ⟶ 3_____

Fighting talk

Miranda Carter woke up one day last summer and told her husband she wanted to be a boxing promoter – someone who organizes boxing matches. It was a suprising career change for a mother of three working in a top job in the civil service but Miranda wasn't joking and later that year she put on her first fight.

Before she joined the civil service she used to be a trade union representative. She also used to work for a charity, so what made her decide on this unusual second career? In Britain, women didn't use to work in boxing and while there are more female boxers now, there aren't many women fight promoters. Maybe it's in the family. Her father, Frank, used to do some boxing in the navy before he joined the civil service. Miranda never saw him fight, but remembers him talking about it. 'I recall my father talking about what a difference boxing made to his life', she says. 'He was an aggressive man but boxing used to help him to control his emotions'. He didn't use to take her to boxing matches and she never saw him fight but he used to talk about fights he was involved in.

The same qualities that helped Miranda get to the top of the civil service are helping her succeed in boxing and she's determined to keep her new company – *Left Jab* – in the business of boxing.

2 Complete these sentences. Choose the correct answers.

1 Miranda *used to / didn't use to* be a trade union representative.

2 Women *used to / didn't use to* work in boxing in the UK.

3 Her father *used to / didn't use to* fight.

4 Frank *used to / didn't use to* take Miranda to see boxing matches.

5 He *used to / didn't use to* talk about his fights with her.

3 Complete each of these sentences with one verb in the past tense and one verb with *used to*.

1 Esme _____ (enjoy) skiing, but she _____ (give up) after she broke her leg.

2 I _____ (learn) to type when I was 16 but at the time I _____ (think) it was a useful skill.

3 Organizations _____ (worry) about people working from home but now this _____ (not be) the case.

4 Jeremy _____ (be) never good at managing his workload; he _____ (say) there wasn't enough time in the day.

5 The weather _____ (be) really strange last month. It _____ (not be) so hot in February.

4 Write questions for each conversation.

1
a Salwa used to work in another company.
b Really? When _____ our company? (join)

2
a I was very good at sports a few years ago.
b Which sports _____ ? (do)

3
a I used to run quite a lot but I don't run as often now.
b How many kilometres _____ last week? (run)

4
a When I was in America I used to live in New Orleans.
b Really, so did I. Where _____ ? (live)

1 Look at the article opposite and match the headings in the box below with the paragraphs.

> Do your homework   Find someone you know
> Avoid topics that make people angry
> Keep it simple   Ask open questions   Practise!

2 Read the article again and tick (✓) the things you should do or cross (✗) the things you shouldn't do.

1 look for someone you already know ⬭

2 try to be funny ⬭

3 ask open questions ⬭

4 talk about things you don't know much about ⬭

5 talk about religion ⬭

6 practise small talk with lots of different people ⬭

3 Complete this word map with the words in the box.

> designer label   storm   boiling   actor   sales   thriller
> aunt   plot   nephew   in-laws   changeable   suit

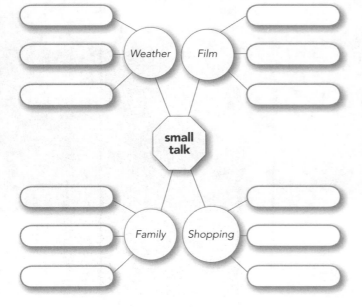

How to make small talk

1 _____

When you enter a crowded room, look for a familiar face and go and talk to them. This will make you feel comfortable. Your friend may be able to introduce you to some of the other people there.

2 _____

The three main topics to avoid are politics, sex, and religion. If one of these topics comes up, it's a good idea to say 'Excuse me' and find someone else to talk to.

3 _____

The people who are best at making small talk are not always those who say the most – they are those who know how to make others feel at ease. When you meet someone for the first time, make a comment about the weather or the place where you are, such as 'This is a lovely house, isn't it?' Then introduce yourself.

4 _____

Find out what's in the news. Then you'll have something to say about whatever topic comes up. Think about things to say, and avoid subjects you don't know much about. This will make you sound informed and interesting.

5 _____

A good way to keep the conversation going is to ask open-ended questions that avoid one-word answers. Don't ask 'Did you have a good day?' say 'Tell me about your day.' The best small talkers are usually good listeners.

6 _____

Practise by talking to people whenever you get the chance. When you're waiting in a shop, talk to the people around you or to the waiter at a restaurant. The more you talk with other people, the easier it is to make small talk.

4 Is each sentence correct (✓) or incorrect (✗)?

1 Henri, you'll never believe the latest new about Grace. _____

2 On today's national headlines, the economic crisis gets better. _____

3 We've heard something about the company takeover. _____

4 Jim told me a news about Greta – she's moving to America next week! _____

> ⚠ *News* is an uncountable noun.
> We can say: *I heard some **news*** or
> *It's an interesting piece of **news***, but not
> ~~I read a **news** about him.~~

5 Correct the mistakes in exercise 4.

1)) **8** Listen to five people greeting each other and complete this table.

conversation	1	2	3	4	5
met before	✓				
not met					

2 Listen again and complete these greetings.

1

Bill: Hey Jim! How's ¹_____?

Jim: ²_____. And yourself?

2

Michael: ³_____ Günther? My name's Michael, from marketing.

Günther: Yes, it is. It's nice to finally ⁴_____ to a voice.

Michael: I've been ⁵_____ to meeting you.

3

Antonio: Sara, it's ⁶_____ again.

Sara: Antonio, it's ⁷_____. So, where are you working now?

4

Xinzhu: Hi, you're Jolanta, the head of personnel, ⁸_____?

Jolanta: Yes, that's right, and ⁹_____ research. It's Xinzhu, isn't it?

Xinzhu: That's right.

5

Marina: Hello, Arjit. ¹⁰_____ you?

Arjit: Not at all. Please take a seat.

3 Match 1–6 with a–f.

1 Yes, it's been a long time since

2 You haven't

3 Hey, what's

4 What are you up

5 Long time

6 Great to see you again too Sandra.

a changed a bit.

b no see.

c new?

d to these days.

e How have you been?

f we met last.

4 Read the compliments (1–14) and put them into groups (a–f).

a Accepting a compliment ⟨11⟩ ⬭

b Responding with a compliment ⬭ ⬭

c Questioning a compliment ⟨3⟩ ⬭

d Sharing the praise with someone else ⬭ ⬭

e Downgrading the praise, so it seems less important ⬭ ⬭

f Giving an explanation ⬭ ⬭

1 Thanks very much. I thought it quite went well too.

2 Oh, it was nothing really – just a few small changes.

3 ~~Do you really think it suits me?~~

4 I'm glad you liked it – I worked hard on it.

5 Well, you know we were very lucky to be asked to do the design in the first place.

6 And you haven't got older at all either since the last time we met.

7 It took us a long time to get it like this – a lot of hard work.

8 Well, it was as much Steve's work as mine.

9 Are you sure – you're not just saying that are you?

10 You look great too!

11 ~~Why thank you, you're very kind.~~

12 The prize is great but it wasn't just me. I had a lot of help from my team too.

1 Complete these definitions. Use one word from the box in each gap.

> passionate   invisible   pioneer
> apprentice   therapy   transform

1 If someone or something is _____ it is not noticed or not talked about.

2 A _____ is someone who is important in the early development of something and whose work or ideas are later developed by other people.

3 _____ is the treatment of an illness or injury over a fairly long period of time

4 Someone who works for an employer for a fixed period of time in order to learn a particular skill or job is an _____ .

5 To _____ is to completely change the appearance, form or character of something or someone, especially in a way that improves it.

6 Someone who has a _____ belief believes something very strongly.

2 Read the article opposite. Complete these notes.

> 1 Number of self-employed people selling
>   The Big Issue: _____
> 2 Street News was started: _____
> 3 Sales per week of The Big Issue: _____
> 4 The cost of a copy of The Big Issue
>   magazine: _____
> 5 The Big Issue was started: _____

3 Look at the article again. Are the sentences true (T) or false (F)?

1 Sellers of *Street News* made 100% profit. ◯

2 John Bird, the editor of *The Big Issue*, had also been homeless. ◯

3 *The Big Issue* sellers pay for the magazine before they sell it. ◯

4 People writing articles for the magazine are not professional writers. ◯

In 1989 in New York, musician Hutchinson Persons founded *Street News*, a newspaper for homeless people to sell. In 1991, Gordon Roddick, a pioneer of social enterprise, was in New York on business when he noticed a man selling *Street News*. Unlike homeless people in London, he was laughing and joking with the customers.

THE BIG ISSUE

This inspired Roddick to start his own paper for the homeless in the UK. He approached John Bird, who had worked in the print trade and who had also been homeless. Roddick knew Bird would be a passionate editor of a street paper. They both believed that the way to solve the problem of homelessness was to help people to help themselves. *Street News* was given away free to the homeless seller, who then sold it for a profit; Roddick wanted to sell the paper to the homeless, who could then sell it on to their customers. *The Big Issue* is a business, not a charity: homeless sellers buy the magazine for 75p and sell it for £1.50. In so doing they learn a business. They take charge of their sales, manage their finances and develop the skills to deal with the public, starting off as apprentices and becoming self-employed business people.

At its launch in September 1991 *The Big Issue* attracted a lot of media attention. It employed professional journalists and has interviewed many famous and important people. It looks like any other commercial magazine but it is a social enterprise. Today it is the most successful street paper in the world, with current weekly sales of over 147,000 copies and 2500 self-employed sellers in the UK. It has helped thousands of homeless people to earn an income and get therapy for health problems associated with homelessness.

The Big Issue is now one of the world's biggest social enterprises with versions of the magazine published in Australia, Japan, South Africa, Kenya, Ethiopia, Malawi and Namibia. Years after its launch, the street paper is continuing to transform the lives of homeless people.

4 Read these definitions and find words in the article to complete this crossword.

1 To start an organization, company, school or city, often by providing the necessary money.

2 To start something, usually something big or important.

3 An organization that gives money, goods or help to people who are poor or sick.

4 All the organizations, such as television, radio and newspapers, that provide news and information for the public, or the people who do this work.

5 To arrange for a book or magazine to be written, printed and sold.

6 Working for yourself and not employed by a company.

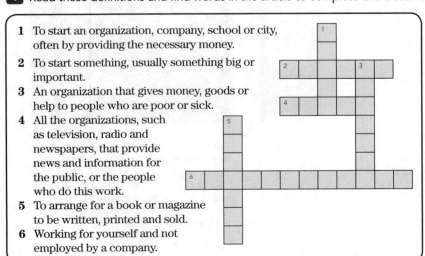

6

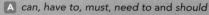

A *can, have to, must, need to* and *should*
B Obligation in the past
C Writing emails 1
D **Communication strategies** Giving advice
E **Interaction** Helping new people

Rule of thumb

A Can, have to, must, need to and should

1 Read the article below. Then choose the correct verbs to complete it.

2 Look at the article again. Are the sentences true (T) or false (F)?

1 It's necessary to find a separate space for your office. ◯

2 You should work only when you want to work. ◯

3 You can start your day with an activity you like. ◯

4 You don't have to behave like your boss. ◯

5 You shouldn't limit the time you work. ◯

3 Rewrite the sentences. Use the verbs in brackets.

1 It is necessary for new staff to attend a training course. (must) _____

2 It is possible for staff to work when they like. (can) _____

3 Visitors are required to sign the Visitor's Book. (have to) _____

4 The right thing to do for Mercedes is to retire now. (should) _____

5 Our employees are not allowed to work at home. (can't) _____

6 It's a really bad idea to try to fix the computer yourself. (shouldn't) _____

4 Read these sentences and choose the correct meaning.

1 The food is lovely – you must try some.
 a I am telling you to do this.
 b I think you will enjoy it.
 c This is the law.

2 You must remember to call Jothy later.
 a I think you will enjoy it.
 b I feel this is necessary.
 c This is a rule.

3 All car drivers must pass a driving test.
 a This is good advice.
 b I think this is necessary.
 c This is the law.

4 Switch off your computer at the end of the day.
 a This is a company regulation.
 b The computer needs a rest.
 c This is the law.

Home offices

Working from home ¹*should / can* seem like a great idea. You ²*don't have to / mustn't* commute and there's nobody checking your work. But working from home isn't all easy – you ³*don't have to / mustn't* fall into the trap of putting things off and leaving them to do another day. You ⁴*should / need to* put some thought into how to get the best out of home working.

Firstly, it's a good idea to set up a separate space in your home as your office so that you ⁵*can / have to* put some distance between home space and work space. Everyone you live with ⁶*should / has to* know this room is your office. This ⁷*should / must* allow you to get on with work without being distracted by domestic life.

It's important to be strict about working hours. Choose the times of day that suit your working habits best. If you're not at your best first thing in the morning, you could do something you enjoy first – take the dog for a walk, perhaps, or go swimming – but then you ⁸*can / have to* get down to work. You ⁹*must / can* make a list of working rules, such as 'no Internet surfing' and 'no personal phone calls during work hours'. Because you're the boss, you need to manage yourself!

Because you're at home you ¹⁰*don't have to / shouldn't* cut into your personal and family time. Set some limits on your work and make sure you enjoy the rest of your life!

1 Match the two parts of the sentences.

1 Because we're going on holiday next week I asked Jim to keep

2 I know the boss is making some bad decisions but just do it to keep

3 Qui isn't very fit. She couldn't keep

4 You know you can't trust Yelda. She never keeps

5 The building site is really dangerous – keep

a an eye on the house.

b her promises.

c him happy.

d out.

e up with me going up the stairs.

2 Read this article and match the headings in the box with paragraphs A–D.

> Quiet!   No breaks   Bad planning   Illness is no excuse

THE WORST BOSS?

If you're reading this at work and you're afraid your boss might be angry because you're reading when you should be working – cheer up, you're not alone! Here are some stories about bosses who are not so perfect.

A _____ Jasmin, an office manager, was asked to organize an employee trip. She planned a picnic two months later. Unfortunately it rained on the day of the picnic. Jasmin's boss was really angry and told her that she had to organize another trip in good weather. Jasmin refused and as a result her boss refused to promote her.

B _____ Tom, a worker in a call centre, had to call an ambulance to take his wife to hospital one morning. At the hospital, the worker called his boss and said he couldn't go to work. The boss said his employee didn't need to stay with his wife because she was with a doctor and he had to come back to work immediately.

C _____ A factory owner told workers they were not allowed to visit the café during work hours except at lunchtime. This meant that staff had to work several hours without a drink or a snack. Workers who needed something to drink or eat received warning letters.

D _____ Carol, a postal worker, had a cold and kept coughing. Her manager criticized her for breaking one of his many rules about a quiet workplace. Among the other things the workers were not allowed to do – sneezing too much and too loudly, singing at work and talking too much.

3 Read the article again and mark each sentence correct (✓) or incorrect (✗).

1 Jasmin's boss said she didn't need to organize another trip.

2 Tom had to take his wife to hospital in his car.

3 Tom's boss said he didn't need to stay with his wife.

4 The factory workers weren't allowed to visit the café during lunch.

5 The postal workers didn't have to to sing at work.

4 Correct the mistakes in exercise 3.

5 Complete this paragraph with *had to*, *needed to*, *was / were allowed to*.

Workers lives in Britain in the nineteenth century were very different from today. Agricultural workers 1_____ to work from sun up to sun down, which meant long days in the summer. Unfortunately in winter they had fewer hours and less pay as they 2_____ the light to work in the fields. When the factory system came in, workers' lives became easier as they only 3_____ work when the machines were working, so they had more regular hours and pay. As workers' rights improved they 4_____ to have Sunday off and later, a half day on Saturday 5_____ as a rest period.

1 Match these punctuation marks with their names.

1	comma	**a**	?
2	full stop	**b**	-
3	semicolon	**c**	Z
4	colon	**d**	_
5	capital letter	**e**	:
6	underscore	**f**	Z
7	dash	**g**	.
8	bracket	**h**	;
9	question mark	**i**	,
10	lower case letter	**j**	)

2 Label the punctuation in the emoticons, which are used in text messages.

1

a _question mark_

(?_?)

b _____

2

a _____   b _____

(-.-)Zzz

c _____

3

a _____   b _____

;-)

4

a _____   b _____

:-(

3 Match the emoticons in exercise 2 with their meanings below.

a joking _____

b surprised _____

c sad _____

d sleepy _____

4 Match these abbreviations with what they stand for and their meanings.

Stands for ...

> thirsty   are you free?   ~~great~~   Laughs out loud
> bye bye for now   can't wait to see you

	Message	Stands for ...	Means ...
1	GR8	great	
2	LOL		
3	RU3		Are you available?
4	1sty?		
5	BBFN		
6	CW2CU		

Means ...

> See you later.   Would you like a drink?   That's very funny.
> ~~Are you available?~~   I really want to meet you.   Good.

> GR8 2CU last
> week, RU3
> on Weds?
> CW2CU,
> BBFN
> Tim

5 Write the text message in full.

6 Read the letter below. Are these sentences true (T) or false (F)?

1 Nguyen knows Ms Kellaway. ◯

2 The writer would like Ms Kellaway's advice about some research she is doing. ◯

3 Nguyen would like to call Ms Kellaway. ◯

> Hi Ms Kellaway!
> I am looking into the way writing styles in emails has changed and want to talk to you about this – I think that you have already done some research into this and guess that this would be a good starting point for a longer chat. If this is acceptable to you, can you let me know when you have a minute so that we could arrange to meet!
> See you soon,
> Nguyen Tran

7 Replace the underlined informal phrases with the phrases in the box.

> are available   understand   researching   could
> would like to discuss this with you   believe   dear
> conversation   I look forward to hearing from you

How to give advice

1. Ask for the facts and try to understand their causes.

2. Explain the reasons behind your advice to the person.

3. Consider the advantages and disadvantages of the different pieces of advice.

4. Think about the problem – does it need action? If so, is it urgent, important or both?

5. Choose the best piece of advice.

6. Give the advice clearly to avoid the person misunderstanding you .

1 Read the steps above for giving advice and put them in order.

①　○　○　○　○　○

2))) **9** Listen to the conversation about moving offices. Choose the correct answers to complete the sentences.

1 Alan wants advice about …

   a creating a positive atmosphere.

   b how to choose rooms for people.

   c when they are going to move.

2 Alan thinks there is …

   a bad office politics.

   b no problem with Mark's first piece of advice.

   c a problem with Mark's first piece of advice.

3 Mark thinks Alan's new idea is …

   a really good.

   b really bad.

   c good but with some problems.

4 Mark suggests that the office workers share rooms according to …

   a their interests.

   b their names alphabetically.

   c their favourite football team.

5 Mark asks Alan to let him know the results because he …

   a wants to forget about it.

   b wants to leave work now.

   c might need to do it again another time.

3 Listen again and complete the sentences with the phases in this box.

> it would be better to   maybe you could
> what you could do is   we might want to   don't do that

Mark: Well, the easiest thing is to let the staff choose. ¹_____ ask everyone to choose their own room.

Alan: Yes, but ²_____ think about planning who shares with who.

Mark: What do you mean exactly?

Alan: The problem I have is office politics. People may choose someone they like this week and next week they might hate them.

Mark: That's true. Have you got any other ideas?

Alan: I thought ³_____ choose people at random, you know, like a lottery.

Mark: No, ⁴_____. You might get a lot of complaints from people who really do dislike each other – even if the system is fair. There might be another option, though.

Alan: Go ahead.

Mark: ⁵_____ ask people to give us a list of interests and try to match them according to this.

Alan: That's good advice. And if that doesn't work, I'll do the lottery idea.

4 Is each sentence correct (✓) or incorrect (✗)?

1 I'm not sure about Anna's some advice about painting the meeting room red.　○

2 Let me give you good advice – don't park your car there. You could get a fine.　○

3 The advice you gave me about cooking steak for last night's meal was useless – everyone was vegetarian.　○

4 Thanks for the piece of advice about buying a new car – I bought it yesterday.　○

> ⚠ Advice is an uncountable noun; you ask for, give, or get *some* advice. Alternatively, you can say *a bit of/a piece of* advice.

5 Correct the mistakes in exercise 4.

Panic attack

It's the first day of your new job. In your old job, everyone and everything was familiar. Here, you don't know anyone and you don't know where anything is. Then you begin to wonder if changing jobs was a good idea and panic sets in. Don't ignore your panic, understand it and control it.

You may be afraid that you misjudged the job and your abilities but you need to remember that you were offered this job based on a selection process, so your employer obviously thinks you have something to offer. Don't judge yourself until you've thought about the new situation and have taken in all the new information.

You shouldn't allow your nerves to get out of control. First, you should realize you're going through change. Your panic will decrease after you enjoy a few successes. For example, you could make yourself speak at your first meeting – it will help you break the ice with your colleagues. Team up with one of your co-workers so they can show you around. Slowly, you will become part of the team and this will help your nerves.

Secondly, what you could do is think about your reasons for taking the job. Remember why you applied for the job, what you didn't like about your last job and what your hopes are for the new job. Ask someone to show you around and compare your new workplace with the old one. You need to get to know your company and not worry about getting things wrong – nobody gets in trouble for making mistakes on their first day.

Finally, review what you expect from this new job. You could draw up a plan of what you expect to happen in the next year. There's no place for panic when you have a plan. Remember, it's up to you to make it work!

1 Match the words and phrases in this box with the definitions below.

> nerves   break the ice   panic   ignore

1 to make people feel more friendly and willing to talk to each other

2 to deliberately pay no attention to something that you have been told

3 the feeling of being worried or a little frightened

4 a sudden feeling of fear that makes you unable to think clearly

2 Look at the article opposite. What does it do?

a gives advice and instruction on how to be successful in a new job

b tells how to make friends and meet people in a new company

c gives advice and instructions on how to deal with nervousness in a new job

3 Complete this table with words and expressions from the article.

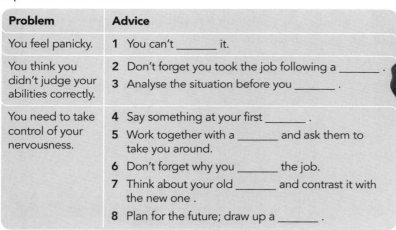

Problem	Advice
You feel panicky.	**1** You can't _____ it.
You think you didn't judge your abilities correctly.	**2** Don't forget you took the job following a _____ . **3** Analyse the situation before you _____ .
You need to take control of your nervousness.	**4** Say something at your first _____ . **5** Work together with a _____ and ask them to take you around. **6** Don't forget why you _____ the job. **7** Think about your old _____ and contrast it with the new one . **8** Plan for the future; draw up a _____ .

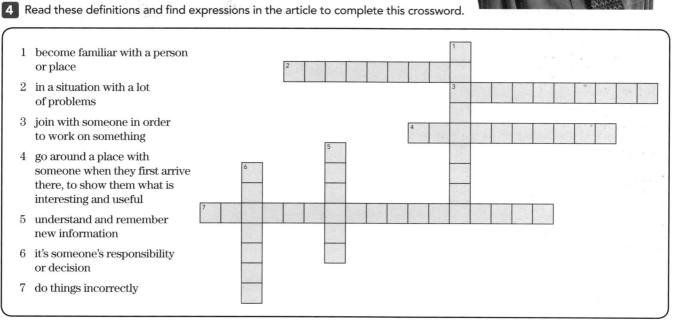

4 Read these definitions and find expressions in the article to complete this crossword.

1 become familiar with a person or place

2 in a situation with a lot of problems

3 join with someone in order to work on something

4 go around a place with someone when they first arrive there, to show them what is interesting and useful

5 understand and remember new information

6 it's someone's responsibility or decision

7 do things incorrectly

Tell us a story

A Past continuous

1 Look at the articles opposite and match these jobs with the people.

a taxi driver
b ice cream parlor assistant
c hospital worker
d drummer

Ben Cohen

Mick Jagger

Madonna

Jerry Greenfield

2 Read the articles again and complete them. Use the correct form of the verbs in brackets.

3 Match the underlined words in the article with the synonyms below.

a boring _____
b left university early _____
c difficult _____
d hopeful _____

4 The sentences a–c below all use the past continuous. Match the sentences with their uses (1–3)

1 actions or situations in progress in the past _____

2 background details or describing longer events (together with the past simple) _____

3 two or more actions in progress at the same time _____

a While he was working as a teacher, he experimented with making his own ice cream.

b At the time he was studying there, Jagger was also working as a porter in a hospital.

c For some time she was not living in very good conditions.

Before they made it

The biggest rock and roll group in the world started in Chelsea, London when Keith Richards and Mick Jagger moved into a flat with guitarist, Brian Jones. While Richards and Jones ¹_____ (make) plans to start their own rock group, Jagger ²_____ (study) business at the London School of Economics. At the time he was studying there, Jagger was also working as a porter* in a hospital. Although he studied for a degree in finance, he ³_____ (finish) it, and instead <u>dropped out</u> to follow a musical career.

When Madonna went to live in New York City in 1977, things were <u>tough</u>. The <u>aspiring</u> future pop star had little money and for some time she was not living in very good conditions. During this time she ⁴_____ (work) at Dunkin' Donuts and dancing with modern dance companies. While she ⁵_____ (perform) as a dancer, Madonna ⁶_____ (become) involved with musician Dan Gilroy and formed her first band, the Breakfast Club, in which she sang and played drums and guitar.

Jerry Greenfield met Ben Cohen at school and their friendship grew over the next few years. Greenfield ⁷_____ (go) to college to study medicine and while he was there he served ice cream in the college cafeteria. In the meantime, Cohen ⁸_____ (follow) his interest in pottery and ⁹_____ (have) a number of <u>humdrum</u> jobs, including a cashier and a taxi driver, before he started work as a teacher. While he ¹⁰_____ (work) as a teacher, he experimented with making his own ice cream. By 1977, Ben decided to go into the ice cream business with his friend Jerry Greenfield, and they opened Ben & Jerry's Homemade Ice Cream Parlor. Today Ben and Jerry's is one of the most famous ice cream brands in the world.

porter: someone whose job is to carry people's bags at railway stations, airports, etc.

1 Read the article below and complete this timeline.

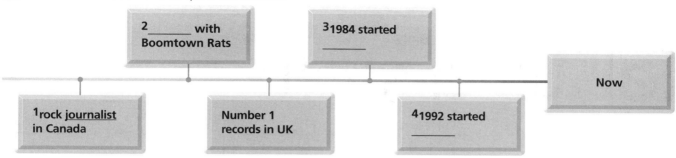

2 _____ with Boomtown Rats

3 1984 started _____

1 rock journalist in Canada

Number 1 records in UK

4 1992 started _____

Now

THE MANY LIVES OF SIR BOB

Sir Bob Geldof has had many lives.
He is co-owner of Ten Alps, a media production company which has grown to around £80m turnover, but he is best known for his charity interests and his music career. Geldof began his career in the media – as a journalist on a rock magazine in Canada. He then returned to Ireland and became a member of the group *the Boomtown Rats*. He hadn't planned on becoming a rock singer – he had originally returned to Dublin to set up his own rock and roll magazine. After a series of hits, including two UK number 1 singles, Geldof starred in the film of Pink Floyd's *The Wall*. After this, in 1984, Bob turned his attention to a famine that was affecting Ethiopia and created Band Aid. Geldof had seen the news about the famine and called other musicians to persuade them to join together to make a hit record *Do they know it's Christmas?* But this wasn't enough for Geldof and he later set up the Live Aid concerts which raised another £150 million. By 1992 Bob Geldof had established himself as a businessman when he began TV production company, Planet 24, which started early morning television in Britain with the show *The Big Breakfast*. Planet 24 was sold in 1999 and the next day Geldof started Ten Alps. In 2005 Geldof organized concerts in eight countries called Live 8. Earlier Tony Blair had invited Geldof to join the 'Commission for Africa' and the Live 8 concerts were staged as a lead up to the G8 meeting of the world's biggest economic countries.

2 Look at the article again and put these events in order (1–6).

a Started Ten Alps media company. ⬭

b Created Live Aid. ⬭

c Saw the news about a famine in Ethiopia. ⬭

d Starred in *The Wall*. ⬭

e Started Live 8 to support the Commission for Africa. ⬭

f Tony Blair invited him to join the 'Commission for Africa'. ⬭

3 Complete these sentences. Use the correct form of the verbs in brackets.

1 Although Ravi _____ (be) now a successful businessman, he _____ (suffer) many business failures before he finally _____ (become) wealthy.

2 The office _____ (be) very quiet this evening. Everyone _____ (go) home early.

3 Jose _____ (not be) at the company very long before he _____ (be) promoted.

4 Janina _____ (go) for the job of sales manager but she _____ (not have) much experience in the area.

5 Why _____ Thiery _____ (not take) the job? _____ he _____ (not read) the job description before he _____ (apply)?

6 a The other people were very well prepared for the meeting. They _____ (know) what we wanted say.

b Do you think someone _____ (tell) them before the meeting?

1 Match the words (1–3) with the expressions on these faces.

1 laugh ◯
2 frown ◯
3 smile ◯

2 Look at the words in the box below. Put the words in order from most to least humorous.

> serious   amusing   hilarious   funny

☺ ————————————————— ☹

1 _____   2 _____   3 _humorous_   4 _____   5 _____

3 Match the words in the box with the definitions below.

> joke   anecdote   irony   comedy   satire

1 a short story based on your personal experience _____

2 something that you say or do to make people laugh, especially a funny story or trick _____

3 when you use words that are the opposite of what you really mean, often in order to be amusing _____

4 a way of criticizing somone or something, by deliberately making it seem funny so that people will see their faults _____

5 entertainment that is intended to make people laugh _____

4 The eight speech bubbles below are from two jokes. Read the jokes and decide which sentences belong to joke A or B.

Joke A The office worker   **Joke B** A poor student

1 (B) A professor was marking the exams he had just given to his class and opened the test of a bad student.

2 ◯ 'Excellent, excellent!' said the manager as his paper disappeared inside the machine. 'I just need one copy.'

3 ◯ A young worker was leaving the office late one evening when he found the manager standing in front of a shredder* with a piece of paper in his hand.

4 ◯ Inside the test were just empty pages and a €100 note. The only thing the student had written on the test was '€100 = 100%. I get an A grade.'

5 ◯ The professor gave the student the exam back. When the student opened it, inside were three €20 notes and the writing '€60 = 40%. You fail!'

6 ◯ 'Listen,' said the manager, 'this is a very important document here and my secretary has gone for the night. Can you make this thing work?'

7 ◯ 'Certainly,' said the young man. He turned the machine on, put the paper in and pressed the start button.

8 ◯ A month later, the student approached the professor. 'I don't understand,' he said. 'I failed the course. Didn't you mark my exam paper?'

*shredder = a machine that tears paper into small pieces.

5 Read the sentences again and put them in order.

Joke A ◯ ◯ ◯ ◯
Joke B ①　◯ ◯ ◯

6 Choose the correct answer to complete the sentences,

1 Filipos is always telling jokes – he's a very fun / funny guy.

2 Going to a comedy club for a night out is lots of fun / funny.

3 A fun / funny thing happened to me on my work today.

4 Well I'm glad you all enjoyed that practical joke but I don't think it's very funny / fun at all.

> ⚠ Don't use fun and funny in the same way.
> Use fun to talk about situations or activities that you enjoy.
> The picnic was (good/great) **fun**. NOT ~~funny~~.
> Funny is used to describe someone or something that makes you laugh.
> The joke was really **funny**. NOT ~~fun~~.

1 Complete the storytelling phrases with the words and phrases in the box.

> kidding similar thing sounds like what happened
> never forget believe about the time reminds

1 And then _____ ?

2 Did I tell you _____ when…?

3 That _____ me of the time (when)…

4 I'll _____ the time…

5 A _____ happened to me when…

6 I don't _____ it!

7 That _____ fun.

8 You're _____ !

2 Put the phrases in exercise 1 into groups.

a starting a story _____ , _____

b showing interest in a story _____ , _____ , _____ , _____

c linking one story to another _____ , _____

3))) **10** Listen to a story and put these pictures in order. Write the letters A–D in these boxes. ◯ ◯ ◯ ◯

4 Listen to the story again and tick (✓) the phrases in exercise 1 that you hear.

5 Complete the story below with the words in this box.

> at the time in the end then so luckily when but

Anyway, they went to the skydiving centre and flew up to around 13,000 feet before the instructor and this guy jumped out of the plane. They were the last two people to jump. After a minute of freefall, the instructor pulled the parachute. [1]_____ the man said 'It's really quiet up here'. After the instructor said 'Yes', he asked the instructor another question. This time, he didn't answer. The guy repeated his question [2]_____ got no answer. [3]_____ he looked up at the instructor, he saw something was wrong. The man didn't know it [4]_____ but the instructor had suddenly had a heart attack, [5]_____ he had to steer the parachute by himself. [6]_____ he remembered television programmes he had seen and steered the parachute from memory. The instructor was dead – but the man managed to land safely [7]_____ in a field three miles away from the airport.

6 Correct the mistake in each sentence.

1 There are three things to remember: never be late to a meeting, always switch off your phone and eventually, don't leave early. _____

2 I had looked everywhere for my shoes but I found them in the washing machine finally. _____

3 And in the end I'd like to show you this graph which shows the overall age of our employees. _____

4 We didn't want to buy a new umbrella but finally we had to because it was raining so hard. _____

> ⚠ We use *eventually* to say that something happens after a long time.
> ***Eventually*** *he told us what had happened.*
> We use *in the end* to say what the result or outcome was.
> *She found them **in the end**.*
> We use *finally* to introduce the last point you want to make in a series or a list.
> ***Finally**, I'd like to end with a story.*

1 Look at the article below and match these headings with the paragraphs.

1 Practise your pitch.

2 Know what your client is interested in.

3 Be enthusiastic.

4 It's not about you.

5 Aim for a second meeting.

6 Keep it real.

2 Read the article again and answer these questions.

1 What is the aim of the first meeting? _____

2 When will your client find out more about you? _____

3 What are two examples of work you could give? _____

4 Why should you show excitement when you're speaking? _____

3 Match the two parts of the sentences.

1 Let me tell you something

2 We love

3 I'm into internet business, which is my

4 We started our new business last year and it's already

5 So, how does E-personnel

6 You may be

7 The best thing

a work?

b thinking 'Yes, but how many people do they have?'

c profitable.

d what we do.

e about E-personnel is we're so easy to use.

f real passion.

g about myself.

4 Complete these sentences with the words in the box.

start up   entrepreneur   consultant   venture   freelancer

1 Our joint business _____ isn't really working – we lost half a million pounds this year.

2 In 1999 we founded a _____ company selling tickets online.

3 Aaron is an accountant but he also works as management _____, giving advice to companies on their finances.

4 Mark Zuckerberg is a great internet _____ – he started the social networking site, Facebook.

5 Don't worry about all the extra work – I've hired a _____ to do some of it part-time.

Creating an effective elevator pitch

Not many people ever sell to customers in an elevator but that doesn't mean you shouldn't have an elevator pitch – a mini-presentation that says what your company does. Read these tips for developing an elevator pitch that can sell your products in under three minutes.

A _____
Your first aim in any sales meeting is to get another meeting. In the limited time you have, you need to interest your client in your company and focus on what makes your company special. Think about what makes your company exciting and relevant to your customer's needs.

B _____
Try to think which things are of most interest to your client – what your service or product can do for them. Your pitch will be more interesting if you understand what your client wants.

C _____
Don't spend too much time talking about your own career – the customer will have time to find out about you later when you are working together.

D _____
Talk about real examples of what you do. Tell your client about a difficult problem you solved or the buyer who was very pleased with your work.

E _____
An elevator pitch is not just a list of facts or figures. You want to move the person to take action and so you have to show them you care. When your client hears the excitement in your voice and sees your enthusiasm for your company in your body language, they will be more likely to call you back again and want to get to know more.

F _____
Speaking clearly shows clear thinking. Even though your elevator pitch is something you do often, you should still go to a coach to get some feedback on how to improve it and practise it as much as possible.

8

A Zero and first conditionals
B Products
C Second conditional
D **Communication strategies** Problem solving
E **Interaction** Planning a green office

Green chic

A Zero and first conditionals

1 Read the article. Then match the first parts of the sentences (1–6) with the second parts (a–f).

1 Your lighting costs will go down

2 If you switch off the computers in a small office,

3 You waste 500,000 litres of water

4 If you recycle your waste

5 You'll save money on heating

6 If your air conditioning is free from dust,

a if your taps are dripping.

b by keeping the temperature constant.

c it will operate more efficiently.

d if you turn lights off when you're not using them.

e you'll save five per cent of your business' turnover.

f you can save around £300 per year.

2 Complete these sentences with the words in the box.

> launch   replace   reduce
>   drive   reuse

1 We will need to _____ our energy consumption by 15 per cent to bring it down to 55 per cent.

2 The government _____ its new policy on green fuel today.

3 Look, don't throw that bottle away. We can _____ it for drinking water.

4 What kind of car do you _____ ?

5 The company is _____ its fleet of cars with new hybrid cars.

Save money by using resources efficiently

If your organization wants to cut costs, one of the best ways of saving money is to be energy efficient. Here are six things your company can do today to reduce spending.

1 Turn off all office equipment when you've finished with it. When a computer is left on all the time, it costs your company over £50 every year. If you switch it off after work you could reduce this to £15 a year. If you work in a small office with ten PCs, you'll save over £300 per year.

2 Turn off lights in empty rooms and replace bulbs with energy saving ones. If you simply turn off lights in rooms and corridors that aren't being used, you'll reduce lighting costs by as much as 15 per cent.

3 Reduce water consumption by turning off taps. A dripping tap can waste 500,000 litres of water per year. Unless you stop it, it could cost your business £400 per year.

4 See if your business waste could earn you money by selling it to another business so that they can use it in their products. When you recycle your waste by selling it to another business, you save five per cent of your business' turnover.

5 If you keep your heating at a constant temperature (and shut all windows and doors), you make your office more energy-efficient. Just increasing your room temperature by one degree sends your heating costs up by eight per cent.

6 If you make sure the cooling systems and air conditioning are clean and free from dust you'll keep them operating at maximum efficiency.

3 Complete these sentences with the verbs in brackets.

1 If you _____ too quickly here, you _____ a fine. (drive/get)

2 When the room temperature _____ 20°C, the air conditioning _____ on automatically. (reach/go)

3 The door _____ if you _____ that green button. (open/push)

4 If the traffic _____ really bad, he usually _____ his car at home and _____ by train. (be/leave/go)

5 Whenever I _____ a spider, I _____ to run away quickly. (see/want)

6 If I _____ now, I _____ this job on time. (not concentrate/not finish)

4 Rewrite the second sentence to mean the same as the first.

1 People who stay in the sun too long may get skin cancer.

If _you stay in the sun too long_ , you _may get skin cancer_.

2 Unless we act now, global warming will become very dangerous.

If _____ , global warming _____ .

3 If you don't have a better suggestion, we'll go with Istvan's proposal.

Unless _____ , we _____ .

4 By making our products eco-friendly, we will increase our number of customers.

If we _____ , we _____ .

5 Switching off the lights in the corridors could save the company £500 a year.

If _____ , we _____ .

1 Look at the advertisements below and match them with these pictures.

(1)

In the USA alone, 25 billion disposable coffee cups are thrown away each year. You might think that the cups themselves could be recycled but in fact they have a plastic coating in order to keep liquid inside them hot, which means they are not biodegradable and will pollute the environment when they are thrown away. *The Steel Cup* is made of aluminium and comes with its own top so it can be used time and time again.

(2)

Taking renewable energy sources to a new level, the *Miniturbine* is an appliance that uses wind power to charge, or put power, into your gadgets.

(3)

Earth Partner Cleaner is an effective organic washing up liquid. The ingredients we use do not harm the item being cleaned, your body or the environment. It cleans many different household surfaces beautifully and comes in packaging that is 100 per cent biodegradable.

(4)

<u>Nightview</u> is one of the brightest garden lights and gives a 2.5 metre diameter of light for up to eight hours. The energy-efficient lights are run from batteries which use eco-friendly solar power to recharge during the day.

2 Read the advertisements and find words for these definitions.

1 the container or material that a product is sold in _____

2 materials, chemicals, etc. that are changed naturally by bacteria into substances that do not harm the environment _____

3 to make air, water, soil, etc. dangerously dirty and not suitable for people to use _____

4 something which does not use a lot of electricity _____

5 not harmful to the environment – used especially about products _____

6 relating to farming or gardening methods of growing food without using artificial chemicals, or produced or grown by these methods _____

7 intended to be used once or for a short time and then thrown away _____

8 a piece of equipment, especially electrical equipment, such as a cooker or washing machine, used in people's homes _____

3 Use *re-* and *-able* to change the meaning of the words in the box.

> charge   fill   use   cycle

1 _____

2 _____

3 _____

4 _____

4 Use the words from exercise 3 to complete these sentences.

1 A battery you can use again and again is _____ .

2 We can _____ an ink cartridge after ink is put back in again.

3 A hybrid car _____ the electricity generated by the brakes when we stop.

4 Marker pens can be _____ with ink and used again instead of buying new ones.

5 Complete these sentences with the words in this box.

> guzzler   energy   waste   carbon   efficient

1 By 2020, all the industrialized nations will have signed up to the _____ offset plan to fight against global warming.

2 Many fish were killed when poisonous _____ substances were released into the river from the factory.

3 Hybrid cars use both petrol and electricity, making them very fuel _____ .

4 My new car only does 20 kilometres to the litre. It's a real gas _____ .

5 The government wants all new homes built in Australia to use a lot less electricity and be more _____ efficient.

1 Read the article about the Segway i2 and answer the questions below.

1 The i2 runs on ◯.

   a petrol

   b electricity

   c solar power

2 It takes ◯ to learn to drive the i2.

   a one week

   b 30 minutes

   c half a day

3 You wouldn't need to worry about parking because the i2 is ◯.

   a an electric vehicle

   b the same size as a motorbike

   c not very big

4 If you had a full charge, you would be able to travel up to ◯.

   a 12.5 miles

   b 24 miles

   c 48 miles

5 You could have difficulties driving the i2 if ◯.

   a you can't stand up

   b you lean right

   c your balance is poor

2 Read the sentences about the i2. Are they fact (F), possible (P) or imaginary (I)?

1 If you leaned left, it would turn left. ◯ *(I)*

2 If you lean to the right, the i2 goes right. ◯

3 You wouldn't have to worry about parking if you went to a busy place. ◯

4 If you see a policeman on a Segway, you'll know what he's riding. ◯

3 Read this article about Green Party policies. Complete the sentences with the correct form of the verb in brackets.

Life under the Green Party

In the few months up to the next election, Christine Donaldson imagines what life would be like for the ordinary person under each party. Today, the Green Party.

Everyone is eco-friendly today but what would the Green Party do if they were to be the next government? First of all, let's look at transport. They say that if they ¹_____ (win) the election they ²_____ (introduce) cycle routes round the city. In addition, they ³_____ (have) free bus travel for people. If you still ⁴_____ (want) to drive into work, you ⁵_____ (pay) a charge for driving into the city and if you ⁶_____ (drive) a large car, there ⁷_____ (be) an extra tax for this.

SEGWAY

Find a Dealer   Guided Tours   Contact Us | Search | →

BUSINESS   PATROL   ROBOTICS   ABOUT SEGWAY   SUPPORT

Imagine a vehicle that moves the way you move: if you leaned left, it would turn left – if you leaned forward, it would accelerate. A vehicle so easy to use you'd only need half an hour if you wanted to learn to drive it. Then imagine a vehicle that you just step on and off when you want to go somewhere and you wouldn't have to worry about parking if you went to a busy place – it's just 48 cm long and 63 cm wide. The Segway i2 Personal Transporter is the most important development in personal transportation since the car. The i2 is an efficient, practical and fun way of getting around – it lets you commute to work or go from job to job at a top speed of 12.5 miles per hour with a range of up to 24 miles. If you wanted to go further, you could charge the battery from a normal electricity supply, or just put it in the boot of your car until you get nearer your destination.

If you want to go places faster, carry more and do more in less time, the i2 is the ideal form of transport. The i2 works with sensors and an onboard computer – when you push the handle forward, the i2 accelerates, if you lean to the right, the i2 goes right. You would possibly have problems steering the i2 if you didn't have good balance when you're standing up but the way it works is very much how humans move.

Segway Personal Transporters are used by a variety of groups from police forces to tourist guides. So now if you see a policeman on a Segway Personal Transporter, you'll know what he's riding.

• **View Full Specs**

• **How Renewable Energy Credits Work (PDF)**

• **All About Segway Inc.'s REC Program (PDF)**

• **View Product Brochure (PDF)**

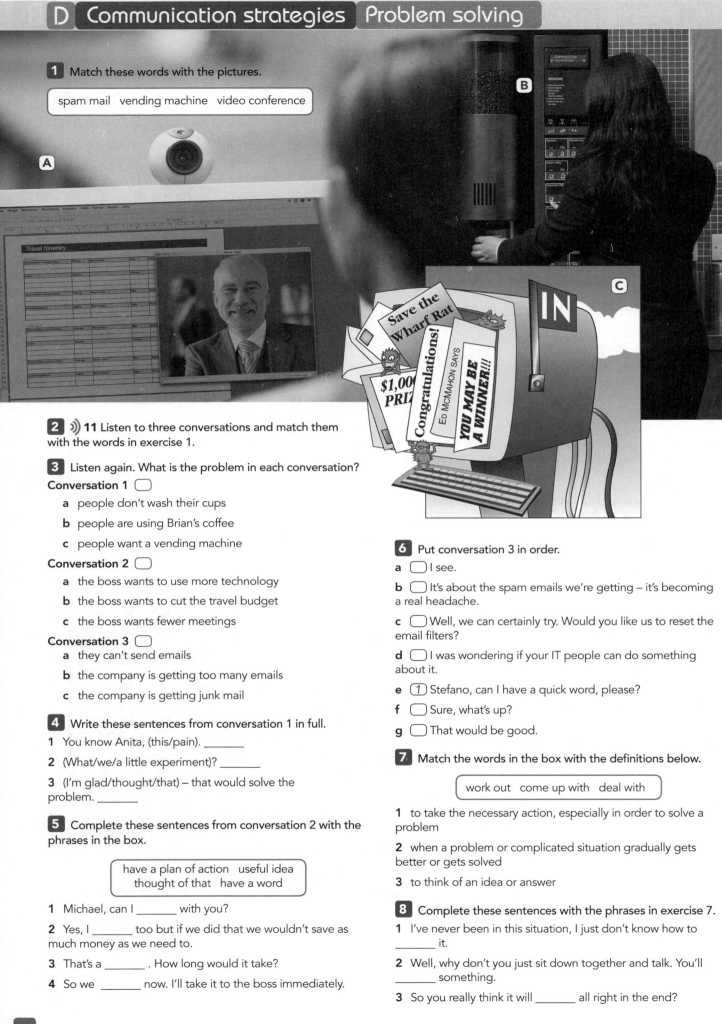

1 Match these words with the pictures.

> spam mail   vending machine   video conference

A

B

C

2))) **11** Listen to three conversations and match them with the words in exercise 1.

3 Listen again. What is the problem in each conversation?

Conversation 1 ○

  a people don't wash their cups

  b people are using Brian's coffee

  c people want a vending machine

Conversation 2 ○

  a the boss wants to use more technology

  b the boss wants to cut the travel budget

  c the boss wants fewer meetings

Conversation 3 ○

  a they can't send emails

  b the company is getting too many emails

  c the company is getting junk mail

4 Write these sentences from conversation 1 in full.

1 You know Anita, (this/pain). _____

2 (What/we/a little experiment)? _____

3 (I'm glad/thought/that) – that would solve the problem. _____

5 Complete these sentences from conversation 2 with the phrases in the box.

> have a plan of action   useful idea
> thought of that   have a word

1 Michael, can I _____ with you?

2 Yes, I _____ too but if we did that we wouldn't save as much money as we need to.

3 That's a _____ . How long would it take?

4 So we _____ now. I'll take it to the boss immediately.

6 Put conversation 3 in order.

a ○ I see.

b ○ It's about the spam emails we're getting – it's becoming a real headache.

c ○ Well, we can certainly try. Would you like us to reset the email filters?

d ○ I was wondering if your IT people can do something about it.

e ① Stefano, can I have a quick word, please?

f ○ Sure, what's up?

g ○ That would be good.

7 Match the words in the box with the definitions below.

> work out   come up with   deal with

1 to take the necessary action, especially in order to solve a problem

2 when a problem or complicated situation gradually gets better or gets solved

3 to think of an idea or answer

8 Complete these sentences with the phrases in exercise 7.

1 I've never been in this situation, I just don't know how to _____ it.

2 Well, why don't you just sit down together and talk. You'll _____ something.

3 So you really think it will _____ all right in the end?

1 Read the article opposite and choose the correct answers.

1 In France most pollution comes from _____ .

   a cars   **b** industry   **c** buildings

2 The building could sell power for as much as €_____ each year.

   a half a million   **b** half a billion   **c** five thousand

3 Most modern offices use _____ kilowatts per square metre.

   a 300   **b** 80–250   **c** 16

4 The building will be about _____ more expensive to construct than an ordinary building.

   a two thirds   **b** a quarter   **c** fifty per cent

2 Look at the article again and answer these questions.

1 How many people can work there? _____

2 Where does the cooling system take water from? _____

3 What keeps the air clean and provides shade for the building? _____

4 What are its main selling points for people to move in? _____

3 Look at the article again and find words which mean the following.

1 system that lets fresh air into a room or building (paragraph 2) _____

2 to use time or energy (paragraph 2) _____

3 material which covers or protects something with a material that stops electricity, sound or heat from getting in or out (paragraph 2) _____

4 the repairs and painting that are necessary to keep something in good condition (paragraph 4) _____

4 Read these definitions and complete the puzzle. Use words from the coursebook. What is the hidden word?

1 to repair a building or old furniture so that it is in good condition again

2 not allowing sound to pass through or into

3 a small part of a room that is separated from the rest of the room

4 to decorate and repair something such as a building or office in order to improve its appearance

5 connected with the environment or its protection

6 the power that is carried by wires and is used to provide light or heat, to make machines work

The world's greenest office block

Many people think that cars are the biggest polluters but that's not true. In France most pollution comes from buildings, the next most pollution is from industry and just under a quarter comes from transport. Commercial property clearly needs greener standards. So now Paris is going to have the world's greenest office building.

The office block, called 'Energy Plus', will be built in Paris. The building will not use any energy because it will produce its own power for heating and lighting, with special ventilation for air conditioning. In addition, after a while it will begin to produce electricity to sell back to the power companies and could sell up to 500,000 euros worth per year. Energy plus will be big enough for 5000 people and will have more solar panels than any other building, while its cooling system will take water from the River Seine and pump it around the offices. Most modern buildings consume between 80 and 250 kilowatts per square metre, while older ones often use up to 300 kilowatts. By using a new type of insulation, the amount of electricity will be reduced to 16 kilowatts per square metre, the lowest in the world for an office block.

The Energy Plus building looks different from standard office buildings, which are generally high-rise towers. This green building will be low-rise with a flat roof for solar panels. Because of the size and shape of the building, more trees can be planted around the building's perimeter to keep the air clean and to shade the building in the summer, further reducing cooling costs.

The building will be 25 per cent to 30 per cent more expensive than a normal building to construct. As tenants will not have to pay for any electricity and maintenance costs will be lower, there will be big savings for any company locating there. There may be one more plus – for companies who market themselves as eco-friendly, Energy Plus is the place to be. ■

9

- A Passive forms
- B Active or passive
- C Telephoning
- D **Communication strategies** Making requests
- E **Interaction** Remote manager

IT Generation

A Passive forms

1 Look at this article. Which gadget in the pictures is the article is about?

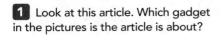

Say Hello to Novelo

The best thing about a book is that it you can forget about everything while you're reading. As you ¹ _____ (take) into the world of the writer, you forget you are reading a book. We wanted to make you forget about Novelo too as you read – just like a physical book – so you can lose yourself in your reading. Novelo ² _____ (design) for reading for long periods of time. Novelo 's buttons for turning the pages ³ _____ (locate) on both sides of the device so that as you read only one hand ⁴ _____ (need) to turn the pages.

For a reading device as good as this, you're going to want a big selection of books. Today, 250,000 books are available on Novelo and can ⁵ _____ (download) in under two minutes. So you can carry your entire collection with you with no extra weight.

Reading the Novelo is a very different experience to reading from a computer screen – the words ⁶ _____ (display) on a black-and-white 15 centimetre screen which looks like real paper and is the size of a real book. Light ⁷ _____ (reflect) from the screen like ordinary paper but unlike ordinary books, when you touch a button the text size ⁸ _____ (increase), making it easier to read in poor light. So with the Novelo, you have all the advantages of a real book and more!

2 Read the article and complete it with the correct form of verbs in brackets.

3 Complete these sentences with the correct form of the passive.

PHONE FACTS

1 Nokia _____ in 1865 in Finland. (found)

2 The world's biggest network provider _____ in China. (base)

3 The first mobile phone call _____ in 1973. (make)

4 The first mobile phone camera _____ by Phillipe Kahn in 1997. (build)

5 Only 20% of all mobile phones _____ in the UK currently. (recycle)

4 Rewrite these sentences. Use the passive.

1 In Britain, people pay £40 a month for their mobile phone bill.

In Britain, £40 a month _____

2 Japanese mobile phone users spend 8.1 hours a month surfing the internet.

In Japan, 8.1 hours a month _____

3 In Santiago City, Philippines, the council has banned mobiles to stop accidents.

In Santiago City, mobile phones _____

4 Teenagers in Korea send an average of 200,000 text messages a year.

200,000 text messages _____

5 Thieves steal one mobile phone every three minutes in the UK.

In the UK, every three minutes _____

6 In the future, scientists would like to place mobile phone cards under the skin of our arms.

In the future, mobile phone cards _____

1 Read the article below and tick (✓) the true sentences.

1 Some employees in Canada are not allowed to use social network sites at work. ◯

2 Over two hours a month are spent at work on Facebook in the UK. ◯

3 Social network sites are said to be a valuable business tool. ◯

4 Facebook members are probably better educated than Bebo members. ◯

Social networking staff given a warning

Workers in Britain, America and Canada are being stopped from viewing interactive social network websites like Facebook. Companies found that wasting office time can ¹_____ by blocking access to social networking sites.

In the past six months, Facebook's British audience has grown 523 per cent to 3.2 million and Facebook has already been banned by some American and Canadian companies. Two months ago, government employees in Ontario were told that social networking sites must ²_____ . Work time can easily ³_____ by staff using sites like Facebook, Bebo and MySpace.

A recent study found that Facebook's British members spend an average of 143 minutes a month on the site checking on their friends, looking up former partners and updating their profile. And it isn't just techies – in the UK around a quarter of workers said they cannot live without using social networking sites at work but is this a problem that must ⁴_____ under control? Facebook is said to be a valuable tool that could ⁵_____ to stay in touch with colleagues and business contacts. People say there is a positive side to social networking that should ⁶_____ by businesses.

Facebook attracts an older audience than MySpace and Bebo. Its members are more likely to be rich, to be better educated and to have more prestigious jobs. Half of Facebook's British members are university-educated and, in comparison to the other sites, it has more professional and executive users.

Copyright © The Times, 2007, www.nisyndication.com

2 Look at the article again and complete the sentences with the verbs in the box.

not access   reduce   waste
use   bring   welcome

3 Match the words with the definitions.

interactive   techie   blog   intranet   podcast   hacker

1 Someone who knows a lot about computers and electronic equipment is a / an _____ .

2 A web page containing information or opinions from a particular person is a / an _____ .

3 A computer network used for exchanging information within a company is a / an _____ .

4 A computer program which does things in reaction to your actions is _____ .

5 A radio programme that can be downloaded from the internet is a / an _____ .

6 Someone who secretly uses or changes the information in other people's computer systems is a / an _____ .

4 Complete these action points from a meeting. Use the verbs in brackets to write full sentences.

Action points from meeting 23 August	
IT issues	**Action points**
1 Connection speed too slow.	The broadband connection _____ by internet provider. (upgrade)
2 Personal data missing.	Next month the computer hard drives _____ . (repair)
3 Junk programmes on hard drives.	Last week all application programmes _____ by IT staff. (check)
4 People watching videos on internet.	Any staff member found watching videos _____ warnings. (give)
5 Company website needs updating.	Recently, all staff involved in our website _____ in design. (train)

5 Decide which sentence sounds best, a or b. Write (F) if it is because the sentence is more formal, or (DK) if we don't know or don't need to know who is responsible for the action.

1 _____

a The government is extending the WiFi network to cover the whole capital city.

b The WiFi network is being extended to cover the whole capital city.

2 _____

a A computer virus has infected our network.

b Our network has been infected.

3 _____

a You have been invited to attend a meeting with personnel.

b We are inviting you to attend a meeting with personnel.

4 _____

a People are being allowed to work at home more often.

b Companies are allowing people to work at home more often.

5 _____

a A thief has stolen important data from the server.

b Important data has been stolen from the server.

C Telephoning

1 Match these phrasal verbs with the correct meaning.

> pick up   speak up   ring up   call back
> put someone through   hold on

1 to say something more loudly _____

2 to lift something or someone up _____

3 used to ask someone on the telephone to wait until the person they want to talk to is available _____

4 to telephone someone again, or to telephone someone because you were not available when they telephoned _____

5 to make a telephone call to someone _____

6 to connect someone to someone else on the telephone _____

2 Read this article and choose the correct phrasal verbs.

GOOD TELEPHONE ETIQUETTE

When answering the phone or making phone calls, good telephone etiquette must be used to give callers a good impression of you and your company.

ANSWERING THE PHONE

Try to ¹*pick up / call back* the phone within three rings (if possible) and always say your name when you answer. Learn to listen without interrupting but if you do have to ²*hang the phone up / put the phone down*, the hold button should be pressed so the caller does not accidentally hear conversations with other people.

TAKING OR LEAVING A MESSAGE

If someone ³*rings up / holds on* and the person they wish to speak to is not there, take a message and let the caller know when the person will be able to return the call. Alternatively, ask them if they want to leave a message on the voicemail before they ⁴*hang up / wait on*. Before you ⁵*speak up / phone someone up*, make sure you know what you want to say. If you have to leave a message for someone, the most important thing is to speak clearly and slowly. Be sure to leave your name and number so they can ⁶*get back to / pick up* you. Keep messages short and cover one topic in one message, saying exactly what you want the person to do or let the person know the best time to ring you back.

3 Match these polite sentences with the correct meanings.

What you say . . .	What you mean . . .
1 She is not at her desk at the moment. Could she call you back?	**a** She is talking to someone else.
2 She is out of the office today. Is anyone else able to help you or would you like to leave a message?	**b** She is busy.
3 She is not available just now. Would you like to leave a message on her voicemail?	**c** I don't know where she is.
4 She'll be back soon. Would you like to leave her a message on her voicemail?	**d** She took the day off.
5 She is in a meeting at the moment. Could you hold on?	**e** She hasn't come in yet.

4 Complete these conversations with the phrases in the box.

> this is Piotr calling from   I'm phoning about
> leave a message after the

Answerphone: Hello, this is IT Generation Software. I'm afraid we're not available right now, but if you leave a message we'll get back to you as soon as we can. Please ¹ _____ tone.

Piotr: Hi, ² _____ the University of Bradford's translation team. ³ _____ the instruction book you wanted translating from Russian into English . . .

> to call me back   it's about   thanks for calling
> away from his desk   to leave him a message

Alan: Hello, is that the after sales department?

Nora: Yes, sir how can I help you?

Alan: ⁴ _____ a virus protection program I bought from you.

Nora: I see. The person who normally deals with software is ⁵ _____ at the moment. Would you like ⁶ _____ ?

Alan: No, not really, but could you ask him ⁷ _____ as soon as he can?

Nora: Certainly, I'll tell him you called. Was there anything else?

Alan: No, that's all thanks.

Nora: ⁸ _____ . Enjoy the rest of your day.

1 Put these words and phrases into the correct group.

> The thing is … That'll be fine. Coming up. It's a possibility. Sorry but …
> I'm afraid … Go ahead. Actually … I'll think about it. No problem.

saying 'yes'

1 _____

2 _____

3 _____

4 _____

saying 'maybe'

5 _____

6 _____

7 _____

saying 'no'

8 _____

9 _____

10 _____

2))) **12** Listen to three conversations and identify the speakers as a, b or c.

a people who know each other well

b people who know each other a little

c people who don't know each other at all

Dialogue 1 ◯   Dialogue 2 ◯   Dialogue 3 ◯

3 Listen again. Which request do you hear, a or b?

Conversation 1 ◯

1 a Send me your design today.

  b Do you think you could send me your design today?

2 a Would it be OK to take your contact details?

  b Can I take your details?

Conversation 2 ◯

3 a Can you call them and ask them for it again?

  b Would you mind asking them again?

4 a Do you mind telling me as soon as you know?

  b Please come back to me as soon as you know.

Conversation 3 ◯

5 a Let's put this payment through quickly.

  b Would you mind putting this payment through quickly?

6 a Do you think you could get me the invoice by tomorrow morning?

  b Get me the invoice tomorrow morning, please.

4 Match the indirect questions with the real meanings.

1 Is anyone sitting there?

2 That music is quite loud, isn't it?

3 This laptop is very old now.

4 What are you doing now?

5 Café Coffee is quite far from here, isn't it?

6 I've left my mobile phone at home.

a Let's go to another café.

b I'd like to sit down.

c I need a new computer.

d Can I use your phone?

e Turn the music down.

f I would like you to do something for me.

5 Correct these mistakes in these sentences. There may be more than one mistake.

1 Sorry, that the latest information isn't available just yet. _____

2 Because of the snow, I'm afraid and all the schools in the area are closed for today. _____

3 I'm sorry, and the kitchen is closed – it's being cleaned at the moment. _____

4 We're sorry but we can't meet you, I'm afraid but we've got another appointment at that time. _____

> ⚠ We say *I'm sorry but …* when we give a reason for saying 'no'. We can also say *Sorry* and then make a new sentence.
> *I'm **sorry**, but I'm very busy at the moment.*
> ***Sorry**. We're closed on Saturdays.*
> We use *I'm afraid (that)* + clause.
> ***I'm afraid** (that) I'm very busy at the moment.*
> ***I'm afraid** you'll have to come back tomorrow.*

WORK IN PROGRESS
SORRY FOR ANY
INCONVENIENCE
CAUSED

1 Match these words in the box to the definitions below. Then find them in the wordsearch opposite.

> multimedia   teleconference
> communication   face-to-face   liaise   trust   isolate
> virtual   initiative   autonomy

1 a meeting in which people in different places talk to each other using telephones or video equipment _____

2 involving computers and computer programs that use a mixture of sound, pictures, video and writing to give information _____

3 a strong belief in the honesty of someone or something _____

4 the ability to make decisions and take action without waiting for someone to tell you what to do _____

5 the process by which people exchange information or express their thoughts and feelings _____

6 to exchange information with someone who works in another organization or department so that you can both be more effective _____

7 made, done or seen on the internet or on a computer, rather than in the real world _____

8 the ability or opportunity to make your own decisions without being controlled by anyone else _____

9 to consider an idea or problem separately from other things that are connected with it _____

10 with another person and talking to them _____

A	F	M	V	R	T	S	M	N	I	L	A	A	C
U	L	N	M	U	L	T	I	M	E	D	I	A	U
T	U	T	Q	R	T	M	P	A	L	Y	A	B	F
O	S	R	S	E	O	O	I	A	R	Y	A	L	A
N	E	U	S	T	V	I	R	T	U	A	L	V	C
O	T	S	I	N	V	X	R	S	V	D	Z	B	E
M	S	T	I	N	I	T	I	A	T	I	V	E	T
Y	N	U	E	E	O	I	I	N	T	I	S	O
E	L	R	P	I	S	O	L	A	T	E	L	B	F
I	M	L	I	A	I	S	E	E	T	I	B	T	A
F	I	B	R	S	T	U	F	S	A	O	C	U	C
T	E	L	E	C	O	N	F	E	R	E	N	C	E
I	I	S	M	O	A	N	A	Y	I	B	L	I	I
C	O	M	M	U	N	I	C	A	T	I	O	N	I

2 Read the article below and choose the correct answers.

1 All need to agree on objectives and on …
  a how many objectives there are.
  b how they should be met.
  c why the remote worker needs to have them.

2 You can keep trust by …
  a frequent criticism.
  b going to meet the remote workers often.
  c helping to solve problems.

3 Teleconferences can be difficult to organize because …
  a technology is needed.
  b everyone is not in the same room.
  c some people are quiet and may be overlooked.

4 Be aware of cultural differences because …
  a there may be difficulties with language.
  b you need to listen well.
  c everyone speaks the same language.

Managing remote teams

Managing people you see every day can be difficult. Think how much more difficult it is when you're managing people on the other side of the world! Brian Jackson manages a team based in Aberdeen, UK and New Delhi. Here he gives some tips on managing remote teams.

Activities can't be directly controlled if the manager is not on the spot. It's essential to agree what the objectives are and how they should be delivered. The next thing to do is create trust, so that everyone in the team believes in the common goals and will work together.

It's easy for trust to break down when team members don't see each other every day. A good way of maintaining trust is to praise people when they do well and respond positively when things are not going so well. People will be more open if their manager responds by helping them solve the problem rather than simply criticizing them.

Well-planned communication is essential. It's important to be in frequent contact by email and phone, of course, but also to go there and have face-to-face meetings with the team. The further away they are, the more important it is that they feel involved and that their contribution is valued.

That may not always be practical, of course, but you can keep in visual touch via teleconferences. These can be difficult to arrange because of the technology involved. The person running the meeting has to observe all the usual meeting rules, making sure everyone has a say and that quieter people are not overlooked, which is more difficult when you're not in the same room and may not hear everything that is said.

Finally, it's important to be aware of cultural differences. People have different ideas of what is expected of them, and of the manager's role. Language difficulties may arise; even if everyone speaks the same language, words can have different meanings in different cultures. If you speak clearly and check that everyone has understood before moving on, it will reduce the possibility of being misunderstood.

10

A Third conditional
B *Should have*
C Collocations
D **Communication strategies** Saying sorry
E **Interaction** Doing the right thing

Right and wrong

A Third conditional

1 Look at the articles and match them with these headlines.

1 100 operations for false doctor ◯

2 Lawyer was a fake ◯

3 14-year-old police officer ◯

CV Fact or fiction?

(A) When **Sam Stevens** applied for jobs at a law firm in Auckland, his application form looked very good. According to his CV, his experience included working in employment law and it said he had a law degree from The University of Wellington. The problem was that he was not a lawyer at all. In fact, Stevens had taken the identity of a New Zealand lawyer who had moved to work in London. Stevens was found out when his boss became suspicious and called the Law Society to check his qualifications. Police say he would have been caught anyway because of his past criminal record if he had continued working as a lawyer.

(B) Swede **Gorin Lindgren** made spelling errors in his CV and produced his own qualifications on his home computer. Thanks to these homemade documents, Gorin got a job as an assistant doctor at a University Hospital. He worked there for more than six months, and took part in over 100 operations. If hospital officials had read his certificates they would have found lots more mistakes. Eventually it was a hospital administrator who checked Gorin's documents as part of an administrative review and found that his qualifications were also false. Gorin was sent to jail for five years.

(C) After a 14-year-old boy spent more than eight hours acting as a police officer, the Denver police department are investigating how this happened. **Ned Spencer** spent two and a half hours driving a police car and went on three assignments. He arrived at the police station in a police uniform bought from a shop but with no police gun or identification. Unfortunately, no one noticed this and Spencer was given a radio and police duties including driving a police car. If nobody had found out that the teenager didn't have a badge or a gun, he would have continued working as a police officer for a lot longer.

2 Read the articles again and find the following.

1 two people who had lied on their CVs. _____ , _____

2 one person with poor spelling. _____

3 one person without correct equipment. _____

4 two people with false university degrees. _____ , _____

3 Match the two parts of these sentences.

1 If he hadn't taken someone else's identity,

2 They wouldn't have found out about Sam

3 If hospital managers had read Gorin's CV more carefully,

4 He wouldn't have done any operations

5 Ned wouldn't have driven a police car

6 He would have continued doing police duties

a he wouldn't have been employed by any law firm.

b if he hadn't had a criminal record.

c if he hadn't dressed up as a police officer.

d if officers hadn't noticed he didn't have a gun or badge.

e they would have found several mistakes.

f if the hospital had known he wasn't a real doctor.

4 Write these sentences in full. Use the third conditional.

1 (If/the company/find out/that Dorota/lie/about her experience, they/fire her) _____

2 (Sheila/get into your car/she/realize/how bad you are at driving) _____

3 (If/I/know/it/get you into trouble/I/put/you in that situation) _____

4 (Would/you/take the job/you/realize/how difficult it/be?) _____

5 (If/you/see/the job advertisement before the closing date,/you/apply for it?) _____

6 (You/believe/how hard he/work to meet the deadline/unless you/see him) _____

1 Read the article below and complete these profiles.

A Cheryl Adamson

1 Won: $_____

2 When: _____

3 Lost money by giving it to _____

B Tom Wilson

4 Won: $_____

5 When: _____

Lost money by   **6** buying _____

                7 lending it to _____

2 Find words in the article which mean the following.

1 a sum of money that a person or organization owes _____

2 let someone borrow money or something that belongs to you for a short time _____

3 relating to money or managing money _____

4 a legal arrangement by which you borrow money from a bank or similar organization in order to buy a house and pay back the money over a period of years _____

5 money in the form of coins or notes _____

6 a payment you make when you buy something that is only part of the full price, with the rest to be paid later _____

3 Read the article again and choose the correct answers.

1 Why did Adamson give money away?
- **a** she owed money
- **b** she wanted to help her friends
- **c** she thought she had too much

2 What happened to the Wilsons?
- **a** their marriage broke down
- **b** they were very happy
- **c** they won the lottery again

3 What does Brady suggest?
- **a** spend the money
- **b** employ an accountant
- **c** don't make any quick decisions

4 What is Adamson's only comfort now?
- **a** she's still alive
- **b** she's was able to help her family
- **c** she felt rich for a while

4 Read these sentences and write criticisms with *should(n't) have.*

1 Adamson always gave money to friends who asked for money. _____ (say 'No')

2 She didn't save any of her money. _____ (save)

3 The Wilsons bought a big house. _____ (not buy)

4 They all started spending their winnings as soon as they got it. _____ (have decision-free zone)

5 A lot of people don't know how to deal with money. _____ (have financial help)

I had it all...

Are you really lucky if you win the lottery? Not necessarily, as one unlucky winner found. Ten years ago, Cheryl Adamson won $6.2 million in the lottery in Ohio, US, and thought that it would change her life. Sadly, she found that winning the lottery wasn't as wonderful as she thought it would be. Today, she has lost it all.

Adamson says that she won and lost the American dream and that it was a very hard lesson to learn. 'Suddenly, I had lots of friends and every one of them wanted some money,' she says. 'I always gave them money – it felt good to be generous.' Adamson says that if she had known then what she knows now, she would have been far cleverer about it. The same thing happened when Tom Wilson won $2.2 million last year. He and his wife Katie put a down payment on a big house and lent their family money to pay off debts. The mortgage, cars and relatives used up all their cash. Now the couple is divorcing and the house has been sold. 'We're worse off than if we had never bought the ticket,' Wilson admits.

Such sad stories are not uncommon. Steven Brady, a financial planner, says that for many people, money arriving suddenly can be a disaster. When a family receives the money, they often find that it causes as many problems as it solves. To stop some bad, early decision-making Brady recommends a DFZ – a decision-free zone. 'A decision-free zone is when you avoid taking any financial decisions, think things through, plan ahead and find help in making important financial choices.'

For Adamson the advice is too late. 'There are a lot of people like me who don't know how to deal with money, because we're not used to having money,' she says. Some people who won the lottery lost all their money in six months. At least I had it for a few years.'

1 Match these words with the correct definitions.

1 blame   **a** something that has been done in the wrong way, or an opinion or statement that is incorrect

2 error   **b** responsible for the effects of your actions and willing to explain or be criticized for them

3 fault   **c** to say or think that someone or something is responsible for something bad

4 mistake   **d** a person's responsibility for what has gone wrong

5 accountable   **e** a formal word used when something has gone wrong, often used when talking about computers

2 Read the article opposite and put these events in order.

a Helena didn't blame the employee. ◯

b The employee lost the files from the project. ◯

c The employee told his manager about the mistake. ◯

d The employee finished the work very quickly. ◯

e The employee expected to be fired. ◯

f The company took responsibility for the error. ◯

3 Look at the article again. Find expressions with *make* and *do*. Complete this table with the expressions.

make	do
a mess	

4 Complete these sentences with an expression with *make*, *take*, *blame*, *be* or *do* and a phrase in the box.

> at fault   someone else   a mistake
> an excuse   the right thing   responsibility

1 Cilla: Look, I really don't want to go to the party tonight.

   Phil: Listen, we'll go for just half an hour then _____ and leave.

2 After Adel had been rude to the customer, he _____ and apologized to her.

3 If you think you can fool your manager with a fake CV, you're _____ .

4 Health and safety is my job and I must _____ for the accident.

5 You can't always _____ when something goes wrong – you're responsible too.

6 Don't take the blame for something Steve did – he _____, not you.

Accountability, not blame

Managers need to understand what the difference is between blame and accountability. Often when a manager says 'We should have more accountability,' they mean 'When things go wrong I really need someone to blame.' Helena Charalombos, a manager in a data protection company, describes how a single event helped her understand the difference between accountability and blame.

'One of my staff came to see me in some distress and admitted he'd made a serious mess of a job he was working on. He was doing some work and accidentally deleted all the files from a project and the client hadn't saved it either. I asked him how much work he had lost and how long he would take to do it again. He said about a week. I thought about it, made my decision and told him to do two things. First, tell the customer exactly what had happened, explain that it was the company's fault and that we would do our best to solve it. Secondly, not to make any excuses, just take care of the problem.

The next day he called to tell me that he had completely redone all the work. I told him that he'd done a good job and that he should give the client the good news. He was amazed that I wasn't going to discipline him or sack him. I told him I don't sack people for making mistakes – I sack them for continuing to make the same mistake.'

Blaming the employee was unnecessary; it would have made him defensive and less likely to learn from the situation. By making him accountable, he learnt from his mistake.

The error wasn't mentioned again and the employee stayed with Helena's company for several years. Blame is about making someone pay the price for mistakes. Accountability is about who is responsible for the results.

1))) **13** Listen and match the conversations with these photographs.

2 Listen again and tick (✓) the things the speakers do.

Conversation	1	2	3
Apologize			
Give an explanation			
Take responsibility			
Not take responsibility			
Show concern			
Offer to put things right			
Respond to an apology			

3 Complete these conversations with the phrases in the boxes.

> really sorry about this   to worry   cause you too many

Conversation 1

1 I'm _____ Mr Abdul but it's not ready yet.

2 I hope it doesn't _____ problems.

3 Not _____. I'll call back this afternoon.

> there was nothing I could do about
> 'm so sorry   I'll get on to it

Conversation 2

4 I _____ – are you OK?

5 I feel really bad about it but _____ it.

6 Sure. _____ right away – oh, and sorry again.

> worry about   I'll check what   accept our apologies for this

Conversation 3

7 I'm very sorry, _____ happened.

8 I'll get someone to come and replace them immediately. Please _____ .

9 Don't _____ it.

4 Complete these sentences with *for*, *about* or *to*.

1 Sorry _____ hear your boss left last week.

2 We're sorry _____ the late arrival of the 4.40 train from Birmingham.

3 Istvan's very sorry _____ saying that your work's not good enough.

4 I'm sorry _____ last night – I forgot my keys and couldn't get in.

5 Sorry _____ bother you but could you pass me that notebook?

6 I'm so sorry _____ what happened to your cat.

5 Match the nouns in the box with the definitions below.

> mistake   complication   fault   error

1 something that has been done in the wrong way, or an opinion or statement that is incorrect _____

2 a mistake _____

3 something wrong with a machine which prevents it from working properly _____

4 a problem or situation that makes something more difficult to understand or deal with _____

1 Match the words in the box with the definitions below.

> wise   thoughtful   open-minded   kind   brave

Someone who …

1 is willing to consider and accept other people's ideas and opinions. _____

2 always thinks of the things they can do to make people happy or comfortable. _____

3 says or does things that show that they care about other people and want to help them or make them happy. _____

4 makes decisions and actions which are sensible and based on good judgement. _____

5 deals with danger, pain or difficult situations with courage and confidence. _____

2 Read the article below and match these figures with what they refer to.

1	240	a	wallets put on the streets
2	0	b	returned wallets with picture of baby
3	88%	c	returned wallets with picture of a family
4	48%	d	wallets containing money
5	20%	e	returned wallets with no picture
6	one in seven	f	returned wallets with charity card

3 Find words in the article to complete these sentences.

1 Zoltan is a very _____ person – he always tells the truth.

2 You know, customer services must be _____ – we should always behave in the same way with everyone.

3 You really believe in aliens and UFOs? I don't think that's _____ .

4 Andrea is very _____ . She always thinks about what people need and tries to help them.

4 How honest are you? Answer this quiz and find out!

1 You see a £10 fall out of a person's coat pocket. Would you:
a stop the person and give it back to them?
b leave it in the street?
c pick it up and keep it?

2 In a store, you knock over an expensive plate and break it. Do you:
a go to the store manager and offer to pay for it?
b say someone else did it?
c leave the store quickly?

3 You buy a ticket for a train with your four-year-old-daughter. The cashier says the journey is free for children under three. Would you:
a tell the cashier your daughter's real age?
b ask if there is a reduced price for children over three?
c buy one ticket only and get on the train?

4 A friend cooks a meal for you but it tastes really bad. Do you:
a tell them their food is terrible?
b say you're feeling quite full but eat a little?
c smile and eat it?

5 Your bank accidentally credits your account with money that isn't yours. Would you:
a tell the bank immediately?
b wait and keep the interest on the money, then return it?
c withdraw the money and hope nobody notices?

Scoring: **a** = 1 point; **b** = 2 points; **c** = 3 points

Want to keep your wallet?

What would you do if you found a wallet on the street? Leave it? Take it to a police station? Post it back to the owner? Keep it? The answer seems to depend more on evolution than on honesty. In an experiment, 240 were put on the streets of Edinburgh.

None of the wallets contained money. Psychologist Richard Wiseman and his team divided them into six groups. In the first four groups, they put a photograph showing a smiling baby, a cute puppy dog, a happy family or an old couple. The fifth group of wallets had a paper saying the owner had made a donation to charity and the final group was a control group* with no photograph or charity papers.

The wallets were dropped on busy streets about a quarter of a mile apart. Overall, 42 per cent of them were posted back. People who picked up the wallet with the photograph of the baby were more likely to send the wallet back. With no picture at all, just one wallet in seven was sent back.

According to Dr Wiseman, 'The baby kicked off a caring feeling in people. This is not just emotional behaviour – it's also very rational. If you find a baby alone, there is a good chance you will look after it and help the survival of the human race.'

The wallets with baby photographs consistently had the highest return rate, with 88 per cent being sent back. Next came the puppy, the family and the old couple, with 53 per cent, 48 and 28 respectively. At 20 per cent and 15, the charity card and control wallets had the lowest return rates.

Whatever the scientific explanation, the message is clear. If you want to increase the chances of your wallet being returned, you should get a photograph of the cutest baby you can find.

a control group: a group used as the standard group to measure changes that may occur in the experiment group.

A Relative pronouns
B Writing emails 2
C Present perfect continuous
D **Communication strategies** Networking
E **Interaction** Team-building

Working together

A Relative pronouns

1 Read the web page below. Are these sentences true (T) or false (F)?

1 Greenpeace was started by people who believe individuals can influence events. ☐

2 It was started because the US was testing submarines. ☐

3 Amchitka is a small city on the coast of Alaska. ☐

4 Greenpeace is based in the Netherlands. ☐

Greenpeace is an international environmental charity

1 _____ was started in 1971. The people who began Greenpeace had a vision of a green and peaceful world and believed a few individuals could make a difference. This was at a time ² _____ the US was testing nuclear weapons on Amchitka, a small island off the west coast of Alaska, ³ _____ some of the last few sea otters and eagles live.

Marie Bohlen, ⁴ _____ was one of the founding members, suggested taking a ship up to Amchitka to oppose the US plans. They organized an old fishing boat to take them there but were stopped by the US navy before they could get to the island. The tests went ahead. However, something had changed – the public, who were not aware of the testing, became interested and this led to the US stopping further tests on the island.

Today, Greenpeace has grown into an international organization ⁵ _____ focuses on global environmental campaigns. Greenpeace, ⁶ _____ is based in the Netherlands, has 2.8 million supporters worldwide and offices in 41 countries.

2 Look at the web page again and complete it with the words in the box.

when   which   where   who   that   which

3 Read the web page again and underline four relative clauses that define someone or something, and three that give extra information.

4 Write these sentences in full using *which, where* or *who*.

1 I gave you the letter. It arrived this morning. *I gave you the letter which arrived this morning.*

2 Jose works in the charity shop. The shop is on High Street.
_____

3 Oxfam is a charity. It is based in Oxford.
_____

4 New Orleans is a city. David comes from there.
_____

5 This the publicity material. Greenpeace sends it out
_____

6 The chef lives in Nice. He won the cooking competition.
_____

5 Put the extra information (1–4), below into this article using correct punctuation and relative pronouns.

> Young children who were affected by the worst nuclear accident in history got a holiday near York. The children visited York as part of a holiday in North Yorkshire. The holiday is for one month. The children from Belarus have an increased risk of cancer from radiation caused by the Chernobyl disaster of 1986. The children from Belarus went to a school for a day of activities.

1 The children are from Chernobyl.

2 The holiday was organized by Friends of Chernobyl's Children.

3 A nuclear power station exploded.

4 They were met by the schoolchildren.

1 Match the words in the box to the definitions below.

> appreciate   hesitate   confirm   coordinate   post

1 to tell someone that a possible arrangement, date, or situation is now definite _____

2 a job, especially an important one in a large organization _____

3 to understand how serious or important someone's feelings are _____

4 to organize an activity so that the people involved in it work well together and achieve a good result _____

5 to pause before saying or doing something because you are not sure _____

2 Read this email and put it in the correct order

> **Subject: Fun Run**

A Mrs J Williams (Heart Australia Fun Run Coordinator)

B ¹ <u>I was wondering if</u> you could confirm your choices for the volunteer posts we have available. There are four posts for which we need volunteers. These are: drinks manager, course managers (two), time recorder. As you know, these are very important in making sure we have a successful Fun Run and ² <u>I would really appreciate an early reply.</u>

C Best Regards,

D ³ <u>Please do not hesitate to contact me should you have any questions.</u>

E ⁴ <u>Dear All,</u>

F ⁵ <u>I am writing to thank everyone for volunteering</u> to take part in the Summer Fun Run in aid of Heart USA, the heart disease charity.

G ⁶ <u>I look forward to seeing you</u> on Sunday for another successful Summer Fun Run.

3 Match the underlined phrases in the email with these less formal phrases.

a If you have any questions let me know. _____

b Thanks for volunteering. _____

c It would be great to get a quick answer. _____

d Can you tell me if … _____

e Look forward to seeing you. _____

f Hello everyone. _____

4 Complete the email below with the phrases in this box.

> Thanks   Hello Jean   See you soon
> Can you tell me if   We all really appreciate

> **Re: Fun Run**

1 _____ ,

2 _____ for the email. As you know I've volunteered to be a Fun Run Official. 3 _____ you still need course managers? It would be great to be the course manager for the final kilometre, but if you already have someone for that, any part of the course would be great.

4 _____ the work you're doing!

5 _____ ,

Lauren

5 Write these phrases in full.

1 (I/forward/see/you) _____

2 (Thanks/advance) _____

3 (I/write/confirm/available) _____

4 (We looking/hearing/you) _____

5 (We/happy/travel arrangements/you) _____

6 (If/questions/please/me) _____

1 Match the words in this box with the photographs.

wedding   engagement   promotion   maternity   retirement

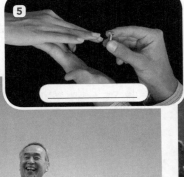

2 Read the newsletter below and answer these questions.

1 Where is the artist from? _____

2 What does Jean want runners to wear? _____

3 Who is the Head of Research working with? _____

4 How long has Christine been living in Adelaide? _____

3 Complete the newsletter with the correct form of the verbs in brackets.

4 Find words in the newsletter which mean the following.

1 to show that an event or occasion is important by doing something special or enjoyable _____

2 a new job within the same organization or another organization _____

3 a move to a more important job or position in a company or organization _____

4 an occasion when there are performances of many films, plays or pieces of music, usually happening in the same place every year _____

NEWS & VIEWS

[**June edition**]

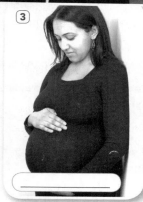

New in-company artist

As part of Arts in Company week, a new artist is making a career move and joining us. Yilun Zhang, from China, 1_____ (make) pottery and ceramics for ten years and 2_____ (work) as an artist in Australia for the past three years. His work is being displayed in reception.

Summer Fun Run

It's that time of year again – we need runners and volunteers for our Fun Run in support of Heart Australia. As part of the Healthy Living festival, Jean Wilson in accounts is organizing the Fun Run. She 3_____ (organize) the event since 2005 and this year she says she 4_____ (encourage) people to run in costumes. Please email her for further details.

Partnership with University announced

Assistant Head of Research, Farhad Alarefi, is pleased to announce a new partnership with Adelaide University. Farhad 5_____ (talk) to the University for the past several weeks about working together and recently the University 6_____ (confirm) our joint business partnership. He's looking forward to promotion to a higher position in the company now.

And finally ...

It's Christine's birthday and time to celebrate. We didn't ask her how old she is but she 7_____ (work) with us for at least five years. She moved to Adelaide six years ago from England and she 8_____ (enjoy) the weather here since then.

1 Complete the sentences below with the correct form of the words in this box.

> liaise   gossip   socialize   enhance   troubleshooting

1 Peter, you shouldn't say such bad things about people, I'm not going to listen to any more of your _____.

2 People are often seen talking together and _____ at work.

3 The publicity from the charity event really _____ his reputation – it's much better now.

4 Can you _____ with Elif – have a meeting or call her – and work on the problem together?

5 **A** Oh no, my PC has frozen again.

B Here, take a look at this _____ guide – you should be able to get it working again.

2 Read the article below. Match the underlined words with these definitions.

1 a person who enjoys or is good at interacting with others _____

2 a person who can help you in business _____

3 the situation of being noticed by people in general _____

4 a large party or official event _____

5 to move from person to person to talk with them _____

Three steps to networking success

Step 1 ▶ Try to go to as many networking <u>functions</u> as you possibly can. Attending networking events will enhance your <u>visibility</u>, especially if you can <u>circulate</u> and introduce yourself to as many people as possible. But make sure you know the difference between networking and gossiping!

Step 2 ▶ Listening to people will get you more <u>contacts</u> in one event than trying to impress people. Try to find out things about them you both share – it shows you are a real <u>people person</u> and are interested in socializing with them.

Step 3 ▶ Try to do someone a favour, offer to help them or do something for them – they'll remember you for it and may help you later. Make sure you get their business card and contact details.

3 🔊 **14** Listen to the conversation and tick (✓) the networking strategies from exercise 2 which Chandra uses.

1 introduce yourself to people ☐

2 find something you both share ☐

3 try to help the other person ☐

4 get their business card ☐

4 Listen again and complete the sentences below with the phrases in the box.

> I don't think met we've before
> how do you know
> I hear she's doing very well
> I know someone at
> are you with   what about you
> perhaps I could help you
> I'd to like in troduce you
> to a colleague

Chandra: Hi, I ¹ _____ . I'm Chandra Raman.

Chandra: Who ² _____ , Philip?

Chandra: ³ _____ Vonnegut's – she's been working there for years.

Philip: So tell me Chandra, ⁴ _____ Helena?

Chandra: We worked together years ago. ⁵ _____ over there.

Philip: And ⁶ _____ ? What do you do?

Philip: I see. Well, ⁷ _____ . Come over here, ⁸ _____ who's been working on internet promotions.

1 Read the article opposite and decide which team-building activities would be good for people who like, or don't like, physical activities.

Like physical activities	Don't like physical activities
abseiling	

2 Read the article again and choose the correct answers.

1 In competitive team building, the losers feel …

 a upset.

 b not equal to the winners.

 c like going home.

2 In competitive team building some members of staff feel …

 a sleepy.

 b like children.

 c bored.

3 Laugher therapy helps …

 a to reduce stress.

 b people deal with their workload.

 c to increase kindness.

4 City hunts involve …

 a police officers.

 b embarrassment.

 c mobile phones.

3 Complete the definitions below with the words in the box.

> incentive   therapy   away day   challenge
> embarrassment   athletic

1 _____ is when you feel nervous, or uncomfortable, especially in front of other people.

2 A _____ is a job or task which is difficult to do or complete.

3 The treatment of an illness or injury over a fairly long period of time is called _____ .

4 Someone who is physically strong and good at sport is _____ .

5 An _____ is something that encourages you to work harder, start a new activity.

6 When a group of people go on an _____ , they leave the office to do activities together.

4 Complete the sentences below with the phrases in the box.

> stretch (their) legs   clear (their) minds   let off steam

1 The problem was so complex, the team had to _____ several times and return to it.

2 Jiying is really angry with her boss. She's talking to Dawn to _____ before she sees him again.

3 I've been sat at my desk all day – I need to go outside and _____ .

One of the team

'TEAM-BUILDING DAY' IS A PHRASE SURE TO WORRY most office workers. In the cause of better cooperation and communication, workers climbed down buildings (abseiling), ran through woods with maps (orienteering) and shot each other with balls filled with paint (paint-balling). Today a new generation of activities is coming soon to an office near you.

These new activities are not as physical as earlier team-building challenges. If there is a competitive element, it is generally not the most important thing, which suggests lessons have been learnt from the past. A recent study found the competitive elements of team building can leave the losers feeling inferior to their more athletic colleagues. Another study found that 68 per cent of office workers disliked traditional team building, and 52 per cent of employees found them 'childish and embarrassing'.

But two new team-building techniques show it doesn't have to be embarrassing. The first, laughter therapy, is a team-building activity for companies who want to encourage teamwork, communication and staff wellbeing. The biggest benefit of it is that stress causes illness and laughter helps reduce stress. It can reduce days off due to sickness but laughing has other advantages too – self-confidence is increased because happy people attract praise. People like to be with happy people.

Even where the competitive and outdoors parts of team building remain, there is a big change from play-fighting or mountain-biking. Take the example of corporate games in cities – the games are citywide adventures, teams of workers use mobile technology to download clues, maps and instructions and communicate with other teams. Actors dressed as ice cream sellers or police officers provide help. It is, according to the company responsible, the future of team building. And like the rest of the new generation of team-building activities, it has one major advantage: office worker embarrassment is greatly reduced. ∎

12

A Reported speech
B Embedded questions
C Consumer vocabulary
D **Communication strategies** Dealing with complaints
E **Interaction** Online entrepreneurs

Trial and error

A Reported speech

1 🔊 **15** Listen to the dialogue between Matt, an accountant, and Francesca, Head of Accounts. Choose the correct answers.

What is Alex Eastman's position?

a accountant

b account team leader

c head of accounts

2 Listen again and answer these questions.

1 How many extra payments were made to the customer?

  a one

  b two

  c three

2 Why is the employee worried?

  a He made the mistake.

  b He didn't do what Alex said.

  c He doesn't want to be responsible for the mistake.

3 Listen again and complete the report form opposite using the correct form of the verb from the conversation.

4 Choose the correct form of the verb to complete these sentences.

1 We've been driving for two hours now. You said that we *will / would* be there in thirty minutes.

2 Hi, Mary. I'm still at work – the boss told me I*'m having / have* to finish the project tonight.

3 Jothy's really worried – the police asked him if they *could / can't* interview him about something.

4 Tim's mother told him that he *must / had to* work harder to pass his exams.

5 Complete these sentences with *say* or *tell*.

1 You're leaving me! But Jean, you _____ me that you loved me!

2 Don't _____ that, Carlos. You knew we could only be together for a short time.

3 _____ me it isn't true.

4 But it is true, I know what I'm _____ to you hurts but maybe we'll meet again someday.

INCIDENT REPORT FORM

From   **Francesca Verdi**

To   **Alex Eastman**

Last week there was an incident reported to me by one of your team.

    One of your team members came to me last Friday and told me that someone ¹ _____ a mistake in one of the accounts the previous week. When I asked what had happened, he said that someone ² _____ two payments – one extra payment – into a customer's account and that nobody ³ _____ . I asked him what he ⁴ _____ about it and he said that when he told you about the mistake, you said that he should not worry about it and that you would tell the staff to be more careful next time.

    However, the employee told me that he ⁵ _____ worried that he ⁶ _____ be blamed for the mistake and came to see me as your line manager to ask me to clarify the situation.

Action: Please contact me to arrange a time to meet.

> ⚠️ After *tell* we say who was told something. So we tell someone something.
> This doesn't happen with *say*. We say something (to someone).
> She **said she** didn't agree.
> She **told the teacher/him** she didn't agree.

1 Read the interview below. What is Beril's job?

> model   actress   singer

2 Put the words in brackets in the correct order to make questions.

1 When and where (happiest/you/are)? _____

2 (do/if/know/this/you) convinced you to become an actress? _____

3 (you/tell/can/me) if you were surprised ? _____

4 (you/could/me/tell) if you are close ? _____

5 (you/when/tell/could/was/me) the last time you cried? _____

3 Put the questions into the interview with Beril.

4 Write the direct questions as embedded questions using *Could you tell me … / Do you think …?*

1 Will you ever get married? _____

2 Will you make another film? _____

3 Would you like to act in action movies? _____

4 Where did your career begin? _____

5 Are you surprised by the success of your movie? _____

6 Is it true that you are dating your co-star? _____

5 The words in this box are from the coursebook. Match them with the definitions below.

> split   scandal   sue   quit   libel   accuse

1 to make a legal claim against someone, especially for money, because they have harmed you in some way _____

2 to say that you believe someone is guilty of a crime or of doing something bad _____

3 to leave a job or school or to stop working on a task without finishing it completely _____

4 to end a marriage or relationship with each other _____

5 an event in which someone, especially someone important, behaves in a bad way that shocks people _____

6 when someone writes or prints untrue statements about someone so that other people could have a bad opinion of them _____

BERIL LEIGHTON INTERVIEW

Beril Leighton has achieved celebrity status playing Glamour Girl's main role. But how does she cope with fame?

(A) _____ *by the popularity of Glamour Girl?*

I can't believe what's happened. It feels like a dream, everything's happened so suddenly.

A tour of Europe changed your life. **(B)** _____ *?*

I was really lost in my career at that time, so I decided to travel. I went to London, Rome, Brussels and Paris. Each day I'd ask myself if what I should do in the future. Eventually, I saw a play at the Globe Theatre in London and thought about acting school. When I got back to the US, I applied to Drama College and the rest is history, really.

You've got a brother called Neil. **(C)** _____ *?*

I see him all the time – he's more than just a brother, he's my best friend too. He's always there when I need him and they're always there for you.

(D) _____ *?*

When my brother got married, I got tearful.

(E) _____ *?*

I love being at home and having friends round. I really like cooking for them and sitting around the flat watching movies together.

1 Read these letters from a newspaper problem page. What is the writer's problem in each letter? Choose from this box.

> having a car repaired getting a refund
> letting an apartment being threatened

Letter 1

Dear Anabelle,

I would like to tell you about a terrible experience I had with a person who said he was a trained mechanic but in fact was a 1 _____ who didn't know his job. When I took my car to him for a simple repair, he asked for money in notes first – 2 _____ . Normally I don't do this but I needed the repair done urgently. Then he told me there was another serious fault with the car. At this point I realized it was a trick and I was being 3 _____. I said I didn't want it doing. Then he came back with an enormous bill, trying to 4 _____ me for the work. I paid the bill but I knew it was too much and when I asked for a part- 5 _____ of about £50, he refused. What should I do now?

Heva

Letter 2

Dear Anabelle,

Recently I saw an advert from a company I thought was 6 _____ and could be trusted. They said that they wanted to be letting agents for a flat I own and if I put my property with them, they would decorate it and rent it to someone. Unfortunately, it was a 7 _____ . I did use them as letting agents but then they employed 8 _____ decorators who made a terrible mess of it and it cannot be rented to anyone now. When I 9 _____ them to the police, one of their people called me and started 10 _____ down the phone at me and made me quite frightened.

Yours,

Manuela

2 Read the letters again and complete them with the words in this box.

> cash in hand overcharge rogue trader
> cowboy refund reported reputable scam
> ripped off screaming and yelling

3 Find words in the letters which mean the following.

1 when things are dirty or not neatly arranged _____

2 to deceive someone in order to get something from them or to make them do something _____

3 to say firmly that you will not do something that someone has asked you to do _____

4 immediately, as a matter of great importance _____

4 Look at these pictures and complete the crossword.

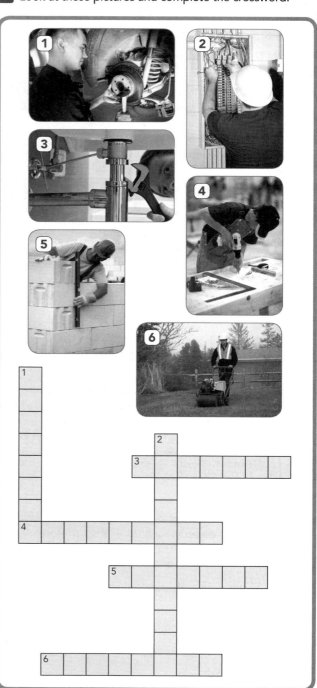

61

1 🔊 **16** Listen to two phone calls and tick (✓) the things the customers complain about.

1 ◯ 2 ◯ 3 ◯ 4 ◯

2 Listen again and complete these customer complaint forms.

Digicam Shop

Customer Services Incident

Name of Customer Service rep: **Jiying Lee**

Name of customer: **1 Jonas Becker**

Order No: **2_____**

Complaint: **Sent wrong 3_____ camera.**

Explanation: **Incorrectly 4_____ at warehouse.**

Action taken: **Offered to 5_____ camera.**

Customer satisfied? **6 Yes / No.**

IT Service Centre
Customer Services Incident

Name of Customer Service rep: Pravin

Order No: 7_____

Name of customer: Muriel 8 _____

Complaint: 9_____ is dead.

Explanation: Battery life depends on 10_____ .

Action taken: Asked customer to look at 11_____ .

Customer satisfied? 12 Yes / No.

3 Complete the sentences below from the phone calls with the phrases in the box.

> really very sorry about this   seems to have been a mistake
> we've been having some trouble
> I'm sorry to hear that   we'll put it right immediately
> completing our customer feedback questionnaire
> how may I help you   if you look at our website

1 Jiying Lee speaking, _____ ?

2 There _____ . I ordered the black camera.

3 Oh dear, _____ . Let me just check back on your order again.

4 I'm afraid _____ with the system.

5 Your order must have been incorrectly processed by our warehouse. _____ .

6 There's just one final thing. Would you mind _____ for our records?

7 We're _____ but I'm afraid we can't do that.

8 _____ , I think you'll find it's out of the guarantee period.

4 Put these phrases for dealing with complaints into the best groups below.

1 You'll need to complete this form.

2 I'm afraid the system doesn't work properly.

3 That must be very annoying.

4 Thanks for letting us know.

5 If you look at our website, sir, I think you'll find …

6 I do apologize.

7 You've made a mistake.

8 I know what you mean.

Showing empathy		
Apologizing		
Correcting and explaining		
Putting things right		

1 Match the words in this box with the definitions below.

discussion forum   business angel
backer   pay-per-click (PPC) advertising
social networking site   chat room

1 a system of marketing where advertisers pay only when someone clicks on their advert _____

2 a place on the internet where people can share ideas and information about a particular subject _____

3 a website where people put information about themselves and can send messages to other people _____

4 a person with money to invest in new businesses _____

5 a place on the internet where you can write messages to other people and receive messages back immediately _____

6 someone who will invest money in a business _____

2 Look at the article opposite and match these questions with the paragraphs.

1 Who can I get investment money from? _____

2 What should I do first? _____

3 What is involved in planning the company? _____

4 What does a good website need? _____

5 How easy is it to start your own business? _____

6 What qualities do people starting an internet business need? _____

7 What are the best ways of marketing my products? _____

3 Read the article and choose the correct option.

1 The first thing to find for your idea is:
 a a strategy
 b a market
 c the competition

2 Your business plan should be:
 a customer-friendly
 b tested
 c well-planned

3 People only buy from websites if:
 a they trust it
 b see something new on it
 c it's expensive

4 Internet businesses should do marketing:
 a in magazines
 b though different internet sites
 c on television

5 Most internet businesses:
 a are successful
 b grow quickly
 c never make a profit

A _____
The internet is a place where individuals can compete with global retailers but how do you get started?

B _____
The first thing you have to do is to find out if there is a market for your idea. Specializing in one section of the market is a good strategy but you need to check if there is any competition first.

C _____
Putting together a business plan means good preparation and research. Who are your competitors? Can you get funding for your idea? How can you build consumer loyalty for your company?

D _____
Your company will need finance. A bank loan is usually the simplest way to do this. Some entrepreneurs have a 'business angel' – a wealthy backer who will invest in a new business and who will also offer help and contacts.

E _____
The cost of a website varies enormously. The key to a good website is to make it safe and easy to use – people will only buy your products if they can easily find what they need and if they trust the site. In addition, you need to maintain and update your site regularly so that customers returning to your site always find something new.

F _____
Internet businesses often fail with their marketing because they do not realize how important it is. Chat rooms and discussion groups are good ways to network and let possible customers know about your store. Pay-per-click advertising is a good way of marketing your products – you pay when someone clicks through to your website after searching for what they want.

G _____
Internet businesses can take a long time to grow and this requires a lot of determination, energy and enthusiasm to keep you going. Many internet businesses never make a profit and success isn't as common as many people think.

4 Find words in the article which mean the following.

1 money that is provided by an organization for a particular purpose _____

2 the quality of trying to do something even when it is difficult _____

3 the quality of remaining faithful to your friends, principles or country _____

4 to make something continue in the same way or at the same standard as before _____

5 to add the most recent information to something _____

Audio scripts

1B, page 5, Exercises 2 and 3

D = Deborah, **S** = Serge

D: Welcome to *The Breakfast Show* on Radio Kelvin, with me, Deborah Singh. Don't you ever think, 'There just aren't enough breaks in my life, with work and home, and not enough time for me'? We've got a special guest here with us today, Serge Taylor, to talk about our work–life balance. We're taking calls as we talk, so for those people who are listening in at the moment the number is 0800 743743. Serge, over to you.

S: Well, I'm starting with a question: What are the most important things in our lives? Usually, it's work and family. We put our energy into the most important things, so when something has to give, the thing that gives is often yourself.

D: But aren't work and family important?

S: Yes, but always remember you're important too. So, why are you neglecting yourself? The answer is often simple – we put other things first. Don't let work and family be the only voices when you are planning. Ask, 'What am I doing for myself today?' and never leave yourself out of the process.

D: Probably a lot of listeners are thinking, 'Why is he telling us this? It's obvious.'

S: But, for people who always put work and family first, this is a real problem. When you are doing any kind of planning, choose to make time for yourself. Choosing is an active process: you don't just hope to find time for yourself, you make time. How about planning your time around you sometimes? You're important too.

D: Sorry Serge, lots of people are probably asking, 'Don't you understand that I have a job? I'm normally busy taking calls, getting things done. I'm working hard at the office. I can't just take a break!'

S: But you're missing something here. Focusing on yourself is not only about taking breaks. It's about putting more of your energy into the jobs you enjoy. Isn't there enough room in your life for these choices? Well, then, it's a pretty good sign that you need to make some serious changes in your life. Now, why am I talking about these issues? My experience is that, when we often ignore important needs, it usually makes our performance poorer. A relaxed and rested person is a more effective person.

1D, page 7, Exercises 2 and 4

C = Christine, **J** = Justin, **B** = Bai Meng

C: So, we've had a good year so far and I'm planning a party for staff to say thank you but we're going to do something a little different. Now here are some ideas – I'd like your thoughts on them.

J: What have we got here then? Fancy dress party, picnic, garden party, dinner party – there are lots to choose from. Bai Meng, what do you suggest?

B: What is a fancy dress party?

C: It's when everyone dresses up as someone or something unusual, for example a film star or a historical person.

B: Well, forget that then – that's just silly.

J: No, no, wait a minute – why don't we think about it first? Fancy dress parties are great fun and some people really enjoy them – they put a lot of effort into their clothes and make up and it can tell you a lot about the person's character you would never guess during work.

C: Perhaps we should consider it in more detail then, Bai Meng.

B: What if we look at all the alternatives? Justin is jumping at the first option. Fancy dress sounds great for people who enjoy that kind of thing but what if you don't? Me, for example.

C: Maybe we could look at the other options then. Let's have a look at this – how about having a dinner party?

J: A dinner party?

B: Good idea – we get dressed up in our formal clothes, black dinner jackets, formal dresses and go for a dinner at a nice restaurant – everyone looks their best.

J: Formal dress! I get dressed formally everyday to come to work – I want to relax in the evenings.

C: Could you take this a bit more seriously, please Justin?

J: Sorry, yes, of course.

B: What if we do something more active? What if we go on a picnic? It's very popular.

C: That doesn't sound very unusual! Can you tell us how you'd make it different, Bai Meng?

B: We all prepare a dish from our own countries or a dish we really like, bring some plates and glasses and choose a nice spot to spend the afternoon.

C: Sounds good to me.

J: Great. What if we offer a prize for the best dish?

C: I think that's a brilliant idea. So have we agreed on a picnic then?

2A, page 9, Exercises 1 and 2

F = Flight attendant, **T** = Turgut,
H = Helen

F: Would you like a hot towel, sir?

T: No, I am okay, thanks. No, actually, I will have one – I've changed my mind.

H: I'll have one too – I've got a long journey ahead.

F: Sure.

T: Are you going to fly all the way over to Singapore too or are you going to land in Zurich?

H: I'm going to go further than that – when I arrive my connecting flight takes me to Sydney.

T: That's tough – Manchester–Sydney. How long is that going to take you?

H: It's about 27 hours. I'll get there at 5:15 on Sunday morning.

T: Is that business or pleasure? My name's Turgut, by the way.

H: Hi – Helen. It's going to be a bit of both really – I'm really going to meet our partner company – they're into mining and we're going to open a joint business in the UK. So I decided to take a holiday and see Australia too.

T: And is your boss OK with that?

H: I am the boss! So the answer is yes – she's happy with that.

T: Have you been there before?

H: No, I haven't. I'm really looking forward to it.

T: What are you going to do out there?

H: I'm not really sure – there are a few places I might visit but I didn't have too much time to plan. So, the answer is that I don't know what I'm going to see when I'm there. I guess I'll decide when I get there.

T: How long have you got? There's a lot to do there. I guess the first place most people head for is Sydney Harbour.

H: Yes, I'm going to go there on the first morning – if I can get out of bed – I'm going to see it with a walking tour.

T: A walking tour? Take plenty of water with you – it'll be really hot at this time of year. When you're in that area try to see the Opera House.

H: That sounds really interesting. I'll try to go there. I've always been interested in music. Any more recommendations?

2D, page 12, Exercises 2 and 3

N = Nirav, **A** = Adèle, **M** = Mary

N: Did you read the article on the world's friendliest countries, Adèle?

A: Yes, I did, Nirav.

N: What did you think about it?

A: I just thought it was silly. What about you, Mary?

M: Actually, I don't agree – I thought it was quite interesting.

N: Me too. It had a good point about Americans finding it difficult to make friends in other countries.

A: OK, Nirav but the article says that it's because the people in the country aren't friendly. I wouldn't say that's true at all – it's easy to make friends when you speak the language – that's why Canada is the top country.

N: I suppose so Adèle but there are other reasons for this too – sometimes the differences in culture can make it difficult for people to make friends.

M: Possibly but many people do make friends in spite of cultural differences. And I think you'll find that if you really try, you can make friends and integrate.

N: Do you really think so, Mary?

M: Absolutely – it's the people who go to the other country who don't try hard enough to make friends.

A: But don't you think there is a more important point, Nirav?

N: What's that?

A: It takes a long time to make friends and when people only stay for a year or two. It's just not long enough to get to know someone. Especially in a country like the UK where people are quite shy.

N: I'm not really sure but the article is very general.

A: Definitely, that's what I mean – it's silly to generalize like that – there are just too many things to take into consideration.

3B, page 15, Exercises 1 and 2

M = Marina, **Y** = Yi Wen

M: Oh, it's lovely here – what a nice restaurant. Thanks for inviting me.

Y: That's quite OK. I often bring people here – it's quite close to the office but it's quiet and the food is excellent.

M: Oh good. Well, I'm looking forward to this.

Y: Great, and we'll have a chat about the new project while we're eating – is that OK?

M: No, that's fine – we don't often talk business over dinner in my country but I'm used to it now.

Y: So, have you eaten Malaysian food before?

M: Oh yes but a long time ago – you'll need to remind me of a few things.

Y: Now, what would you like?

M: Actually, it all looks good. It's a bit difficult to know what to choose.

Y: Can I help you with anything?

M: Yes, please help. What would you recommend?

Y: You must try the fish head curry.

M: Fish head curry – what's that like?

Y: It's a delicacy in Asian cooking and it's more than just the head – it's the top half of the fish. It's very tasty.

M: What does it taste like?

Y: It's spicy.

M: Oh, I can't really eat food that's too spicy.

Y: No, don't worry – it's not going to be too hot.

M: And what's in it?

Y: There's just one fish head in a large bowl depending on its size, with a spoon to take out the curry and get the flesh from the fish head onto individual plates.

M: That sounds good. I'll go with that.

Y: The waiter will put the curry in the middle of the table and you help yourself to the food.

M: OK. What does it come with? Do you eat it with bread?

Y: No, you eat it with rice. You pick up some rice with your first finger, middle finger and thumb and a bit of the fish and curry sauce and eat it that way. Now for the next course – is there anything you don't eat?

Audio scripts

3D, page 17, Exercises 1 and 2

S = Susie, **K** = Kasia

S: Hi Kasia. What are you doing tomorrow evening?

K: Nothing much Susie, I've got a few things to do for work. Why, what's happening?

S: A group of us are going bowling at the Super Bowl – do you want to join us?

K: Oh, I'd love to. I really like bowling but I'm sorry, I can't go. I'm giving a presentation the next day.

S: Can you take a break and come for half an hour? There's someone I'd like you to meet.

K: Er, it sounds like good fun but I don't think I can. I need to concentrate on my presentation tonight.

S: Oh, OK Kasia. I won't insist but it's a pity.

K: By the way Susie, who do you want to introduce me to?

S: It's just a friend – I think you'll like him.

K: I'm really sorry but I have to practise and I don't feel like meeting new people at the moment – I've got too much stress with this presentation.

S: It's OK, I understand. You don't have to come.

K: Look, thanks for inviting me anyway. Let's arrange another time, at the weekend, maybe?

S: And can I bring my friend?

K: All right, you can bring him, if you insist!

4D, page 22, Exercises 2 and 3

A = Angela, **L** = Luca

A: Luca, I'm glad I've seen you. Have you got a minute? I'd like to talk to you about the Head of Marketing's visit.

L: OK. Is there a problem, Angela?

A: Well, we've worked out most of the details of her visit but we have a slight problem.

L: And what's that?

A: Well, you know she's arriving in about an hour?

L: Yes …

A: Well, the room we booked isn't available now.

L: What do you mean it isn't available?

A: It's being decorated – we can't use it now.

L: But she'll be here in an hour! Have you got any suggestions?

A: I was actually thinking of another room. What if we use one of the computer rooms?

L: Oh no, I don't think that would work. Could we check the availability of the reception area – could we have an informal meeting there?

A: I did that and it's not available either.

L: OK, so what are we going to do?

A: How about booking the restaurant over the street? It's got a nice big room for parties and so on.

L: That's a good suggestion. Yes, I'll go along with that and why don't we tell her that's what we planned all along?

A: Yes and I could ask the restaurant to make it a special occasion for her.

L: Great idea. And we could ask the managing director to come too.

A: OK, I'll go to see if she's free now and call the restaurant.

L: Great – let me know what happens. I don't want any more improvisation!

5D, page 27, Exercises 1 and 2

1

Bill: Hey Jim! How's it going?

Jim: Not bad. And yourself?

2

Michael: Is it Günther? My name's Michael, from marketing.

Günther: Yes, it is. It's nice to finally put a face to a voice.

Michael: I've been looking forward to meeting you.

3

Antonio: Sara, it's good to see you again.

Sara: Antonio, it's been a long time. So, where are you working now?

4

Xinzhu: Hi, you're Jolanta, the head of personnel, aren't you?

Jolanta: Yes, that's right, and you're in research. It's Xinzhu, isn't it?

Xinzhu: That's right.

5

Marina: Hello, Arjit. Mind if I join you?

Arjit: Not at all. Please take a seat.

6D, page 32, Exercises 2 and 3

A = Alan, **M** = Mark

A: Mark, glad I've seen you. Have you got a minute? I'd like to ask you for some advice about the move into our new offices.

M: OK, Alan – is there anything in particular you want to ask about?

A: Yes. I wondered how I'm going to choose the rooms for people. We're getting very close to moving now.

M: Well, the easiest thing is to let the staff choose. Maybe you could ask everyone to choose their own room.

A: Yes, but we might want to think about planning who shares with who.

M: What do you mean exactly?

A: The problem I have is office politics. People may choose someone they like this week and next week they might hate them.

M: That's true. Have you got any other ideas?

A: I thought it would be better to choose people at random, you know, like a lottery.

M: No, don't do that. You might get a lot of complaints from people who really do dislike each other – even if the system is fair. There might be another option, though.

A: Go ahead.

M: What you could do is ask people to give us a list of interests and try to match them according to this.

A: That's good advice. And if that doesn't work, I'll do the lottery idea.

M: OK, why don't you go ahead and do that then? And let me know what happens. I'm interested in the results of the move, in case we do it again in the future.

A: Of course. Thanks for the advice – I'm going to explain to our colleagues how we are going to manage the move right now.

7D, page 37, Exercises 3 and 4

H = Helena, P = Paul

H: So your colleagues gave you a gift voucher to drive a racing car and you crashed it!

P: I did – so embarrassing.

H: That reminds me of a story I heard on the news.

P: Oh yes?

H: Did you hear about the guy who got a gift voucher for Christmas but it went terribly wrong?

P: No, what happened to him?

H: It all started when he got a gift voucher from his girlfriend – it was for skydiving with an instructor.

P: Skydiving?

H: Yes – jumping out of a plane, falling through the air, then using a parachute.

P: That sounds like fun.

H: Anyway, they went to the skydiving centre and flew up to around 13,000 feet before the instructor and this guy jumped out of the plane. They were the last two people to jump. After a minute of freefall, the instructor pulled the parachute. Then the man said something like 'It's really quiet up here,' and the instructor said 'Yes'.

P: OK.

H: A few seconds later and he asked his instructor another question. This time, he didn't answer. The guy repeated his question but got no answer. When he looked up at the instructor, he saw something was wrong.

P: And then what happened?

H: The man didn't know it at the time but the instructor had suddenly had a heart attack, so he had to steer the parachute by himself.

P: You're kidding!

H: No.

P: And he had never done it before?

H: Never – luckily he remembered television programmes he had seen and steered the parachute from memory.

P: Did they get down OK?

H: Well, no – the instructor was dead – but the man managed to land safely in the end in a field three miles away from the airport.

P: That's an incredible story. Did I tell you about the time when …

8D, page 42, Exercises 2 and 3

Conversation 1

B = Brian, A = Anita

B: You know Anita, this is a real pain.

A: What's that, Brian?

B: Every time I want a cup of coffee I find that my coffee jar is empty. People are using my coffee instead of bringing their own.

A: I know what you mean – look here, no coffee.

B: What if we do a little experiment?

A: Like what?

B: We can ask everyone to give 30p every time they make a coffee and then use the money to buy a jar for everyone to use.

A: That's a good idea – but we still have to buy the coffee. What if we asked for a vending machine?

B: I'm glad you thought of that – that would solve the problem.

Conversation 2

D = Dieter, M = Michael

D: Michael, can I have a word with you?

M: Sure thing.

D: The boss wants everyone in marketing to be more eco-friendly and is trying to find ways of cutting the travel budget.

M: I see.

D: Any ideas?

M: The simplest thing would be to cut the number of trips.

D: Yes, I thought of that too but if we did that we wouldn't save as much money as we need to.

M: Another idea would be to cut down on travelling for business meetings.

D: That's interesting – go on.

M: We could use video conferencing to do eighty per cent of our meetings and some of our sales.

D: That's a useful idea. How long would it take?

M: It can be brought in very quickly.

D: So we have a plan of action now. I'll take it to the boss immediately.

Conversation 3

L = Lara, S = Stefano

L: Stefano, can I have a quick word, please?

S: Sure, what's up?

L: It's about the spam emails we're getting – it's becoming a real headache.

S: I see.

L: I was wondering if your IT people can do something about it.

S: Well, we can certainly try. Would you like us to reset the email filters?

L: That would be good.

S: Then we could look at setting up new email accounts for people who are badly affected.

L: I like that idea but try the spam filters first and if it doesn't get better within a week we will try the second solution.

Audio scripts

9D, page 47, Exercises 2 and 3

Conversation 1

C = Carlo, **R** = Rep

C: Hello, I'm looking for a price on 100 presentation folders for a conference.

R: Yes, that's fine. What size are the folders?

C: Normal paper size – A4 – but we want our own design on them.

R: No problem. Do you think you could send me your design today so we can give you a price?

C: Sure.

R: Would it be OK to take your contact details?

C: Certainly – the name's Carlo Ricci and the number is …

Conversation 2

C = Carlo, **V** = Viola

C: Viola, has the quote from the print company come in yet?

V: No, I don't think so.

C: Can you call them and ask them for it again?

V: Sure.

C: And please come back to me as soon as you know.

V: Sure thing.

Conversation 3

A = Accountant, **C** = Carlo

A: Hello, Finance.

C: Hi, it's Carlo in marketing and promotions.

A: Ah yes, how can we help you Mr Ricci?

C: I need to make a payment very quickly for the conference next month. Would you mind putting this payment through quickly?

A: Well, you know we have to follow certain rules.

C: But this is an important job.

A: They all are, Mr Ricci.

C: Yes, but this is for the sales conference next month.

A: OK, we'll try our best. Do you think you could get me the invoice by tomorrow morning?

C: Thanks, and do you mind sending me an email confirming when the payment is made?

A: Yes, of course.

10D, page 52, Exercises 1 and 2

1

C = Computer Doctor, **M** = Mr Abdul

C: Hello, Computer Doctor.

M: Hello, it's Mr Abdul from Ryko Trading. I'm calling about the repair to my laptop.

C: Just a minute and I'll see if it's done.

M: OK.

C: I'm really sorry about this Mr Abdul but it's not ready yet.

M: It's still not ready?

C: No, we had to wait for a part to come.

M: But you told me that it would be ready this morning.

C: Yes, if we had the part but we had to order it from the manufacturer and it came this morning – I'm afraid there was nothing we could do about it.

M: Do you know when it will be ready then? I really need it today.

C: I can't promise anything but we'll try to get your laptop ready for this afternoon – I hope it doesn't cause you too many problems.

M: Not to worry. I'll call back this afternoon.

2

B = Ben, **J** = Jacqui

B: What on earth!

J: I'm so sorry – are you OK?

B: Yes, but look at my car!

J: I'm really sorry but a cyclist turned onto the road. I tried to avoid him and I didn't see you there.

B: You mean you couldn't stop in time and you didn't look.

J: Look, it's my responsibility – I feel really bad about it but there was nothing I could do about it.

B: There is something you can do – you can call the insurance company.

J: Sure. I'll get on to it right away – oh, and sorry again.

3

A = Annie, **G** = Geoff

A: Good morning, Copyserve.

G: Hi, this is Geoff Edwards from the High School.

A: Yes, how can we help you?

G: Look, your company serviced all the school's photocopiers last week and now two of them are already broken.

A: I'm very sorry, I'll check what happened – I know the person who did the service has only recently joined us.

G: Well, that's OK but what about our photocopiers?

A: I'll get someone to come and replace them immediately. Please accept our apologies for this.

G: Don't worry about it.

11D, page 57, Exercises 3 and 4

C = Chandra, **P** = Philip

C: Hi, I don't think we've met before. I'm Chandra Raman.

P: Good to meet you, Chandra. Sinclair, Philip Sinclair.

C: Who are you with, Philip?

P: I work for Vonneguts, in market research.

C: I knew someone at Vonneguts – she's been working there for years. Her name's Helena Noble.

P: Let me think – that name seems familiar. Is that the Helena who got married recently?

C: Yes, that's right.

P: Of course I know Helena. Her name's Helena Moore now. So tell me Chandra, how do you know Helena?

C: We worked together years ago. I hear she's doing very well over there.

P: Yes, she was promoted again recently– very good at troubleshooting when problems come up suddenly. She's departmental manager of Research and Development now.

C: Really, that's so cool.

P: And what about you? What do you do?

C: I'm in product development, like Helena.

P: Sounds interesting but why did you come to a sales networking function?

C: We're always looking for new and interesting ways to bring new products onto the market and that's why I thought I'd come here today.

P: I see. Well, perhaps I could help you. Come over here, I'd like to introduce you to a colleague who's been working on internet promotions – she would be very happy to liaise with you on any future projects.

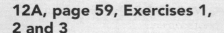

12A, page 59, Exercises 1, 2 and 3

M = Matt, **F** = Francesca

M: Can I see you for a minute, please Francesca?

F: Sure, what's the matter?

M: Someone made a mistake in the accounts last week.

F: What's happened?

M: Two payments were made to a customer. One of them was extra but no one noticed.

F: And what did you do about this?

M: Of course I told Alex but he said I shouldn't worry and that he would tell the staff to be more careful.

F: OK.

M: But I'm worried that I'll be blamed for the mistake and I'd like you to make the situation clear with Alex.

F: OK, I'll complete an incident report now and arrange a meeting with him later this week.

12D, page 62, Exercises 1 and 2

Call A

Jy = Jiying, **Jo** = Jonas

Jy: Hello, Customer Services. Jiying Lee speaking, how may I help you?

Jo: I'm calling about the camera you sent me.

Jy: Can I take your name and order number, please?

Jo: My name's Jonas Becker and the order number is … wait a second, yes it's here – 812697.

Jy: I'll just find you on our system. [A longish pause] I do apologize, sir. Our system is running very slowly at the moment. [Another pause] OK, I've got you here, sir. What seems to be the problem?

Jo: There seems to have been a mistake. I ordered the black camera and the one you sent is silver.

Jy: Oh dear, I'm sorry to hear that. Let me just check back on your order again. [pause] Yes, I can see that now. I'm afraid we've been having some trouble with the system. Your order must have been incorrectly processed by our warehouse. We'll put it right immediately.

Jo: OK, great.

Jy: We'll send out another box for you to send back the silver camera, and as soon as we have received it, we'll send out the replacement black camera.

Jo: And do I have to pay anything?

Jy: No, sir. It's free.

Jo: Thanks very much.

Jy: No problem, sir, and once again I do apologize for the mistake.

Jo: OK.

Jy: There's just one final thing. Would you mind completing our customer feedback questionnaire for our records?

Jo: Yes, I'll do that now.

Jy: Thank you and have a good day.

Call B

P = Pravin, **M** = Muriel

P: Hello, Customer Services. How may I help you?

M: It's about the replacement battery for my laptop.

P: And what seems to be the problem?

M: Well, it's not working any more – it's dead.

P: Oh, I see. Let me take your order number and name.

M: It's order number 47455772 and my name is Muriel Bailet.

P: 47455772. And could you spell your last name?

M: B-A-I-L-E-T.

P: Thanks. So you bought the battery from us four months ago and you also bought a new keyboard.

M: That's right and the battery is already dead, so I'd like you to send me a replacement.

P: We're really very sorry about this but I'm afraid we can't do that.

M: What do you mean? The battery you sold me is faulty. It doesn't work.

P: I'm sure that's the case, madam but the battery life depends on how much you use the computer.

M: What do you mean? I only bought it four months ago. It should last longer than that and there's a six-month guarantee with it.

P: I'm afraid not. The keyboard has a six-month guarantee but the battery only has a three-month guarantee with it. If you look at our website, I think you'll find it's out of the guarantee period.

M: That's ridiculous. I want to speak to the manager.

P: I'm afraid he's not available at the moment, madam but if you can give me your details I'll pass on your complaint and he'll get back to you.

M: OK.

P: In the meantime, would you like to buy a new battery to replace the old one?

M: What?

Unit 1

A

Ex 1
1 25
2 45 minutes
3 2006
4 4
5 40–50 hours

Ex 2
1 a dancer
2 twice a week
3 publicity and marketing
4 charity events
5 spending time with friends

Ex 3
1 hasn't danced
2 was travelling
3 go
4 didn't have
5 has opened
6 is planning
7 learnt
8 is organizing
9 doesn't think
10 is going to be

B

Ex 1
1 a

Ex 2
Serge asks questions 1, 2 and 3.

Ex 3
1 c
2 b
3 a and b

Ex 4
1 present simple
2 present continuous
3 present continuous
4 present continuous
5 present simple

Ex 5
1 It's usually work and family.
2 I'm normally busy taking calls.
3 When we often ignore important needs, it usually makes our performance poorer.
4 But always remember you're important too.
5 The answer is often simple.
6 Never leave yourself out of the process.

Ex 6
1 is, speaking
2 'm coming
3 's happening / 's happened
4 is
5 Does, move
6 are working
7 Are, causing
8 try
9 Do, know
10 is
11 Are, trying
12 'm (still) waiting
13 'm hoping / hope
14 Is, staying

C

Ex 1
1 AAC
2 AAC
3 AAC
4 EFC
5 EFC
6 AAC, EFC
7 AAC, EFC
8 EFC

Ex 2
1 exhilarating
2 stunning, spectacular
3 amazing, incredible

Ex 3
1 c, b
2 b
3 c, c, b
4 a
5 a

Ex 4
play: tennis, video games. badminton
do: sudoku puzzles, crossword puzzles, aerobics, yoga, boxing
go: cycling, skiing, walking, swimming

D

Ex 1
1 come up with
2 Has, share
3 generated
4 submit
5 run out of

Ex 2
A dinner party
B picnic
C fancy dress party

Ex 3
1 what do you suggest
2 why don't we think about it
3 we should consider it
4 Maybe we could look at
5 How about having
6 Could you take this
7 Sounds good to
8 think that's a brilliant

Ex 5
Incorrect: 2, 3, 5

Ex 6
2 If Wednesday is fine with everyone, I propose ~~to~~ meeting then.
3 Didn't Nadira suggest ~~to~~ seeing a film next week?
5 What do you recommend ~~to~~ having from the menu this evening?

E

Ex 1
1 c
2 d
3 a
4 b

Ex 2
1 T
2 T
3 F
4 F
5 T
6 F

Ex 3
a CW
b TW
c TW
d CW
e TW

Ex 4
Across
2 lack
4 fatigue
5 inability
6 interrupt
Down
1 procrastination
3 prioritize

Unit 2

A

Ex 1
Turgut – Singapore
Helen – Sydney

Ex 2
1 27
2 holiday
3 doesn't know
4 walking
5 Opera House

Ex 3
1 a
2 b
3 c
4 c
5 b
6 a

Ex 4
1 is going to
2 'll
3 are not going to
4 will
5 won't
6 is going to

Ex 5
Incorrect sentences: 1, 3, 4, 6

Ex 6
1 a long journey
3 Aiko travelled across Australia
4 a trip to the coast
6 I'm going to travel to China

B

Ex 1
1 T
2 T
3 F
4 F
5 T
6 F

Ex 2
1 are staying
2 will like
3 will be
4 will ride
5 will meet
6 will visit
7 will be
8 will get

Ex 3
1 Will you book
2 Is the bus tour leaving
3 Will you help me
4 are you coming too
5 How much will it cost now
6 Where are you going

C

Ex 1
Facilities offered: 2, 5, 6, 7, 9

Ex 2

1 all the same
2 good value rooms
3 in the room
4 window
5 lighting and music
6 likes

Ex 3

1 five-star
2 power shower
3 king-size
4 room service
5 honeymoon
6 palmtop
7 flatscreen
8 business centre

Ex 4

1 honeymoon
2 flatscreen TV
3 king-size
4 five-star
5 room service
6 power
7 business centre
8 palmtop

D

Ex 1

most friendly: Canada, Germany, Australia
least friendly: China, India, United Arab Emirates

Ex 2

1 Adèle
2 Nirav
3 Adèle
4 Nirav
5 Mary
6 Adèle

Ex 3

1 Actually
2 good point
3 wouldn't say
4 I suppose so
5 Possibly
6 Do you really think so
7 Absolutely
8 don't you think
9 not really sure
10 Definitely

Ex 4

	Informal	Formal
Agreeing	Sure. Uhuh.	I think so. You've got a good point.
Uncertain	Maybe.	I'll have to think about that.
Disagreeing	Yes, but… No way!	Actually, I think you're wrong there. Sorry but I don't agree.

Ex 5

Incorrect sentences: 1, 3, 4

Ex 6

1 I agree with you
3 I think so too
4 I agree

E

Ex 1

A 1 (Sharjah)
B 3 (Al Ain)
C 4 (Abu Dhabi)
D 2 (The East Coast Tour)

Ex 2

Derek: Sharjah
Aylin: Abu Dhabi
Francesca: East Coast

Ex 3

B	J	V	O	B	T	B	L	L	H	U	W	S	W	Y
A	F	Q	Q	G	X	C	Z	O	F	I	D	A	B	K
R	K	P	Q	O	A	S	I	S	A	H	S	N	E	K
B	C	A	M	P	S	I	T	E	J	Z	S	D	L	X
E	W	W	A	R	W	G	S	K	H	D	G	B	L	O
C	B	J	R	P	R	E	O	T	K	H	P	O	Y	D
U	C	X	O	H	N	A	U	Z	T	O	Z	A	D	E
E	R	I	Y	E	Y	Z	K	C	V	W	V	R	A	S
S	D	U	N	E	B	A	S	H	I	N	G	D	N	M
Q	I	T	G	S	I	S	N	W	J	V	N	I	C	T
C	H	H	G	N	C	Q	I	L	S	L	U	N	I	M
H	J	U	J	K	E	Q	F	T	Q	I	T	G	N	M
A	R	C	H	I	T	E	C	T	U	R	E	L	G	F
E	O	E	H	Y	T	I	Q	K	P	U	D	G	F	S
L	E	I	S	U	R	E	F	A	C	I	L	I	T	Y

Unit 3

A

Ex 1

1 ✗
2 ✗
3 ✓

Ex 2

1 Adding
2 tasting
3 to ask
4 eating
5 switch off
6 stare
7 eating / to eat
8 to request

Ex 3

1 having
2 Eating
3 eating / to eat
4 to pass
5 to pay / to go
6 to leave
7 having

B

Ex 1

1 b
2 c
3 c

Ex 2

1 the new project/business
2 It's a delicacy in Asian cooking/it's very tasty.
3 spicy food/hot food
4 with their fingers

Ex 3

1 for inviting me
2 would you like
3 recommend
4 must try
5 like
6 does it taste
7 can't really eat
8 what's in
9 sounds good
10 help yourself
11 come with
12 is there anything

Ex 4

1 e
2 f
3 d
4 a
5 b
6 c

Ex 5

1 rare
2 sparkling
3 steamed
4 strawberry

Ex 6
1 spicy
2 salty
3 delicious
4 chewy
5 rich

C

Ex 1
1 d
2 c
3 a
4 e
5 b

Ex 2
1 much
2 a little
3 too much
4 lots of

Ex 3
1 many
2 much
3 much
4 many
5 much

Ex 4
1 over 7000
2 a little
3 a little
4 lots
5 a lot

Ex 5
1 any
2 too much
3 enough
4 not enough
5 a few
6 any

D

Ex 1
1 Susie asks Kasia about her plans.
2 Susie invites Kasia to go bowling.
3 Kasia makes an excuse.
4 Susie gives Kasia a reason to take a break from work.
5 Kasia asks about Susie's friend.
6 Kasia says *No* again.
7 They arrange to meet another time.

Ex 2
1 do you want to join us
2 I'd love to
3 I don't think I can
4 I won't insist
5 I understand
6 if you insist

Ex 3

Hesitate
Er, Oh

Apologize
I'm sorry I can't go
I'm really sorry but

Suggest an alternative
Let's arrange another time
Perhaps we could meet again another time?

Say something positive
It sounds like good fun but
I really like bowling

Say thank you
Thanks for inviting me anyway
Thank you for thinking of me

Ex 4
1 d
2 f
3 a
4 b
5 c
6 e

E

Ex 1
Acceptable: 1, 2, 3, 7
Unacceptable: 4, 5, 6, 8

Ex 2
1 It is not allowed.
2 So that the person does not appear greedy.
3 So that the person will not show any disappointment.
4 The word for *four* sounds similar to *death* in Cantonese.

Ex 3
1 greedy
2 taboo
3 decline
4 sever
5 tricky
6 gesture
7 extravagant
8 embarrass
Key expression:
good fortune

Unit 4

A

Ex 1
1 both
2 AJ
3 EP

Ex 2
1 can't
2 is able to / can
3 was able to
4 can't / isn't able to
5 are able to

Ex 3
1 could / was able to, wasn't able to / couldn't
2 wasn't able to / couldn't
3 able to
4 can / is able to, can't / isn't able to
5 was able to
6 could / was able to, can't / am not able to

B

Ex 1
1 for
2 of
3 pressure
4 able
5 attention
6 problem

Ex 2
1 computer literate
2 analytical
3 conscientious
4 self-confident
5 resourceful
6 logical

Ex 3
1 f
2 a, c
3 b, d
4 a, e

Ex 4
incorrect sentences: 1, 4, 5

Ex 5
1 has got a very good job
4 That sounds like a nice job
5 after she lost her last job

U	B	R	E	S	C	E	U	T	A	L	R	M	R	F
F	U	E	T	E	M	O	T	I	V	A	T	E	D	M
E	S	L	E	R	F	E	R	V	I	N	V	A	U	P
F	N	I	N	X	U	I	I	E	L	E	L	E	E	P
F	U	A	E	S	U	V	F	E	F	U	E	O	T	I
I	R	B	E	L	F	S	T	L	U	T	F	L	S	U
C	T	L	V	A	U	T	B	T	E	E	U	E	E	E
I	S	E	L	F	S	U	F	F	I	C	I	E	N	T
E	N	U	N	P	U	N	C	T	U	A	L	B	S	E
N	V	S	M	N	F	A	F	E	T	T	L	F	I	B
T	R	E	S	O	U	R	C	E	F	U	L	P	B	L
U	E	F	L	E	X	I	B	L	E	S	L	E	L	U
P	E	R	S	U	A	S	I	V	E	R	M	S	E	T
L	E	U	S	N	U	M	E	R	A	T	E	F	C	S

C

Ex 1

a diploma, PhD
b one-to-one, in-service
c self-study, online
d intensive, part-time
e professor, lecturer

Ex 2

a online, blended e-learning
b instructor, trainer
c extensive, full time

Ex 3

1 F
2 T
3 F
4 T

Ex 4

1 quickly
2 lower
3 shortest
4 better
5 faster
6 most popular
7 greater
8 rapidly

Ex 5

1 more flexible
2 more relaxing
3 more quickly
4 cheaper
5 most important
6 biggest

D

Ex 1

Skills and activities involved:
1, 3, 4, 5, 7, 8

Ex 2

1 available
2 computer
3 reception
4 restaurant
5 managing

Ex 3

1 What if we use
2 Could we
3 How about
4 Yes, I'll go along with that, why don't we
5 Great idea.

Ex 4

Making suggestions:
It might be a good idea to …
Let's …
Could we …?
Why don't we …?

Agreeing with and building on ideas:
I'll go along with that.
Yes, and …
Sounds good to me.
Great idea.

Ex 5

1 might be an idea if
2 and what about if
3 Sounds good to me
4 I will go along with

E

Ex 1

1 b
2 a
3 c

Ex 3

Scores
40–60: You always stand up for yourself but may be aggressive sometimes.
20–40: You are quite assertive and not usually aggressive. You are also respectful of other people.
10–20: You are too passive and let other people make decisions for you and/or control your life.

Ex 4

1 mediate
2 improve
3 assist
4 adapts
5 deal with
6 consider

Unit 5

A

Ex 1

1 TV aerials
2 computer
3 e-m@iler

Ex 2

1 T
2 T
3 F
4 T
5 T

Ex 3

1 He sold TV aerials in the past.
2 He has owned a consumer electronics company since 1968.
3 He bought Betacom and Viglen in the 1990s.
4 He sold his shares in the football club in 1994.
5 Since 2005 he has starred in a television show.

Ex 4

1 is
2 was
3 developed
4 joined
5 has played
6 has also done
7 helped
8 has worked

B

Ex 1

1 civil service
2 trade union representative
3 boxing promoter

Ex 2

1 used to
2 didn't use to
3 used to
4 didn't use to
5 used to

Ex 3

1 used to enjoy, gave up
2 learnt, didn't use to
3 used to worry, is not
4 was, used to say
5 was, didn't use to be

Ex 4

1 did she join
2 did you use to
3 did you run
4 did you use to / did you live

C

Ex 1

1 Find someone you know
2 Avoid topics that make people angry
3 Keep it simple
4 Do your homework
5 Ask open questions
6 Practise!

Ex 2

What you should do: 1, 3, 6
What you shouldn't do: 2, 4, 5

Ex 3

weather: changeable, storm, boiling
film: plot, thriller, actor
shopping: designer label, suit, sales
family: in-laws, nephew, aunt

Ex 4

Incorrect sentences: 1, 2, 4

Ex 5

1 Henri, you'll never believe the latest news about Grace.
2 In today's national headlines, the economic crisis gets better.
4 Jim told me some news about Greta.

D

Ex 1

met before: 1, 3, 5
not met before: 2, 4

Ex 2

1 it going
2 Not bad
3 Is it
4 put a face
5 looking forward
6 good to see you
7 been a long time
8 aren't you
9 you're in
10 Mind if I join

Ex 3

1 f
2 a
3 c
4 d
5 b
6 e

Ex 4

a 1, 11
b 6, 10
c 3, 9
d 8, 12
e 2, 5
f 4, 7

E

Ex 1

1 invisible
2 pioneer
3 therapy
4 apprentice
5 transform
6 passionate

Ex 2
1 2500
2 1989
3 147,000
4 £1.50
5 1991

Ex 3
1 T
2 T
3 T
4 F

Ex 4
1 found
2 launch
3 charity
4 media
5 publish
6 self-employed

Unit 6

A

Ex 1
1 can
2 don't have to
3 mustn't
4 need to
5 can
6 should
7 should
8 have to
9 can
10 shouldn't

Ex 2
1 T
2 F
3 T
4 F
5 F

Ex 3
1 New staff must attend a training course.
2 Staff can work when they like.
3 Visitors have to sign the Visitor's Book.
4 Mercedes should retire now.
5 Our employees can't work at home.
6 You shouldn't try to fix the computer yourself.

Ex 4
1 b
2 b
3 c
4 a

B

Ex 1
1 a
2 c
3 e
4 b
5 d

Ex 2
A Bad planning
B Illness is no excuse
C No breaks
D Quiet!

Ex 3
Incorrect sentences: 1, 2, 5

Ex 4
1 Jasmin's boss said she had to organize another trip.
2 Tom didn't have to take his wife to the hospital in his car.
5 The postal workers weren't allowed to sing at work.

Ex 5
1 had to
2 needed
3 had to
4 were allowed
5 was allowed

C

Ex 1
1 i
2 g
3 h
4 e
5 f
6 d
7 b
8 j
9 a
10 c

Ex 2
1 a question mark, b underscore
2 a capital letter, b lower case letter, c full stop
3 a semi-colon, b bracket
4 a colon, b dash

Ex 3
a 3
b 1
c 4
d 2

Ex 4

	Message	Stands for ...	Means ...
1	GR8	great	Good.
2	LOL	laugh out loud	That's very funny.
3	RU3	are you free?	Are you available?
4	1sty?	thirsty?	Would you like a drink?
5	BBFN	bye bye for now	See you later.
6	CW2CU	can't wait to see you	I really want to meet you.

Ex 5
Great to see you last week, are you free on Wednesday? Can't wait to see you, bye bye for now.

Ex 6
1 F
2 T
3 F

Ex 7
Dear Ms Kellaway,
I am **researching** the way writing styles in emails has changed and **would like to discuss this with** you. I **understand** that you have already done some research into this and **believe** that this would be a good starting point for a longer **conversation. If** this is acceptable to you, **could** you let me know when you **are available** so that we could arrange to meet.
I look forward to hearing from you,

D

Ex 1
Correct order: 1, 4, 3, 5, 6, 2

Ex 2
1 b
2 c
3 b
4 a
5 c

Ex 3
1 Maybe you could
2 we might want to
3 it would be better to
4 don't do that
5 What you could do is

Ex 4
Incorrect answers: 1, 2

Ex 5
1 I'm not sure about Amna's advice about painting the meeting room red.
2 Let me give you some / a piece of advice – don't park your car there. You could get a fine.

E

Ex 1
1 break the ice
2 ignore
3 nerves
4 panic

Ex 2
c

Ex 3
1 ignore
2 selection process
3 judge yourself
4 meeting
5 colleague / co-worker
6 applied for
7 workplace
8 plan

Ex 4
1 get to know
2 in trouble
3 team up with
4 show around
5 take in
6 up to you
7 get something wrong

Unit 7

A

Ex 1
a Ben Cohen
b Jerry Greenfield
c Mick Jagger
d Madonna

Ex 2
1 were making
2 was studying
3 didn't finish
4 was working
5 was performing
6 became
7 went
8 was following / followed
9 had
10 was working

Ex 3
1 humdrum
2 dropped out
3 tough
4 aspiring

Ex 4
1 c
2 a
3 b

B

Ex 1
1 journalist
2 singer
3 Band Aid
4 Planet 24

Ex 2
a 4
b 3
c 2
d 1
e 6
f 5

Ex 3
1 is, had suffered, became
2 was, had gone
3 had not been, was
4 went, had not had / did not have
5 didn't take, hadn't he read, applied
6 knew, had told

C

Ex 1
1 b
2 a
3 c

Ex 2
1 hilarious
2 funny
3 humorous
4 amusing
5 serious

Ex 3
1 anecdote
2 joke
3 irony
4 satire
5 comedy

Ex 4
A 2, 3, 6, 7
B 1, 4, 5, 8

Ex 5
A 3, 6, 7, 2
B 1, 4, 8, 5

Ex 6
1 funny
2 fun
3 funny
4 funny

D

Ex 1
1 what happened
2 about the time
3 reminds
4 never forget
5 similar thing
6 believe
7 sounds like
8 kidding

Ex 2
a 2, 4
b 1, 6, 7, 8
c 3, 5

Ex 3
B, C, D, A

Ex 4
That reminds me of …
That sounds like fun.
And then what happened?
You're kidding!
Did I tell you about the time when …?

Ex 5
1 Then
2 but
3 When
4 at the time
5 so
6 luckily
7 in the end

Ex 6
1 switch off your phone and finally, don't leave early
2 I found them in the washing machine eventually / in the end
3 And finally I'd like to show you
4 eventually / in the end we had to

E

Ex 1
A 5
B 2
C 4
D 6
E 3
F 1

Ex 2
1 To get another meeting.
2 When you start to work with them.
3 A difficult problem you solve, a customer who is pleased with your work.
4 To move your client to take action on what you've said.

Ex 3
1 g
2 d
3 f
4 c
5 a
6 b
7 e

Ex 4
1 venture
2 start up
3 consultant
5 entrepreneur
6 freelancer

Answer key

Unit 8

A

Ex 1
1 d
2 f
3 a
4 e
5 b
6 c

Ex 2
1 reduce
2 launches
3 reuse
4 drive
5 replacing

Ex 3
1 drive, will get
2 reaches, goes
3 opens, push
4 is, leaves, goes
5 see, want
6 don't concentrate, won't finish

Ex 4
1 If you stay in the sun too long, you could / might get skin cancer.
2 If we do not act now, global warming will become very dangerous.
3 Unless you have a better suggestion, we'll go with Istvan's proposal.
4 If we make our products eco-friendly, we will increase our number of customers.
5 If we switched off the lights in the corridors, we could save the company £500 a year.

B

Ex 1
1 d
2 a
3 b
4 c

Ex 2
1 packaging
2 biodegradable
3 pollute
4 energy efficient
5 eco-friendly
6 organic
7 disposable
8 appliance

Ex 3
1 rechargeable
2 refillable
3 reusable
4 recyclable

Ex 4
1 rechargeable
2 reuse
3 recycles
4 refilled

Ex 5
1 carbon
2 waste
3 efficient
4 guzzler
5 energy

C

Ex 1
1 b
2 b
3 c
4 b
5 c

Ex 2
1 I
2 F
3 I
4 P

Ex 3
1 won
2 would introduce
3 would have
4 wanted
5 would pay
6 drove
7 would be

D

Ex 1
A video conference
B vending machine
C spam mail

Ex 2
1 vending machine
2 video conference
3 spam mail

Ex 3
1 b
2 b
3 c

Ex 4
1 this is a real pain
2 What if we do a little experiment?
3 I'm glad you thought of that

Ex 5
1 have a word
2 thought of that
3 useful idea
4 have a plan of action

Ex 6
1 e
2 f
3 b
4 a
5 d
6 c
7 g

Ex 7
1 deal with
2 work out
3 come up with

Ex 8
1 deal with
2 come up with
3 work out

E

Ex 1
1 c
2 a
3 b
4 b

Ex 2
1 5000
2 The River Seine
3 trees
4 low maintenance or electricity costs, it is eco-friendly

Ex 3
1 ventilation
2 consume
3 insulation
4 maintenance

Ex 4
1 refurbish
2 soundproof
3 cubicle
4 renovate
5 green
6 electricity
Key word: energy

Unit 9

A

Ex 1
b

Ex 2
1 are taken
2 is designed
3 are located
4 is needed
5 be downloaded
6 are displayed
7 is reflected
8 is increased / increases

Ex 3
1 was founded
2 is based
3 was made
4 was built
5 are recycled

Ex 4
1 is paid / spent on mobile phone bills.
2 is spent surfing the internet.
3 have been banned to stop accidents.
4 are sent by Korean teenagers each year.
5 a mobile phone is stolen.
6 will be placed under the skin of our arms.

B

Ex 1
1 ✓
2 ✗
3 ✓
4 ✓

Ex 2
1 be reduced
2 not be accessed
3 be wasted
4 be brought
5 be used
6 be welcomed

Ex 3
1 techie
2 blog
3 intranet
4 interactive
5 podcast
6 hacker

Ex 4
2 is being upgraded / is going to be upgraded
3 will / are being / are going to be repaired
4 were checked
5 will be given
6 have been trained / were trained

76

Ex 5

1 b (DK)
2 b (DK)
3 a (F)
4 a (F)
5 b (DK)

C

Ex 1

1 speak up
2 pick up
3 hold on
4 call back
5 ring up
6 put someone through

Ex 2

1 pick up
2 put the phone down
3 rings up
4 hang up
5 phone someone up
6 get back to

Ex 3

1 c
2 d
3 b
4 e
5 a

Ex 4

1 leave a message after the
2 this is Piotr calling from
3 I'm phoning about
4 It's about
5 away from his desk
6 to leave him a message
7 to call me back
8 Thanks for calling

D

Ex 1

1 That'll be fine.
2 Coming up
3 Go ahead.
4 No problem.
5 It's a possibility.
6 Actually, …
7 I'll think about it.
8 The thing is …
9 Sorry but …
10 I'm afraid …

Ex 2

1 c
2 a
3 b

Ex 3

1 b
2 a
3 a
4 b
5 b
6 a

Ex 4

1 b
2 e
3 c
4 f
5 a
6 d

Ex 5

1 Sorry, ~~that~~ the latest information isn't available just yet.
2 I'm afraid ~~and~~ all the schools in the area are closed
3 I'm sorry, ~~and~~ **but** the kitchen is closed
4 I'm afraid ~~but~~ we've got another appointment.

E

Ex 1

1 teleconference
2 multimedia
3 trust
4 initiative
5 communication
6 liaise
7 virtual
8 autonomy
9 isolate
10 face-to-face

Ex 2

1 b
2 c
3 a
4 a

A	F	M	V	R	T	S	M	N	I	L	A	A	C
U	L	N	M	U	L	T	I	M	E	D	I	A	U
T	U	T	Q	R	T	M	P	A	L	Y	A	B	F
O	S	R	S	E	O	O	I	A	R	Y	A	L	A
N	E	U	S	T	V	I	R	T	U	A	L	V	C
O	T	S	I	N	V	X	R	S	V	D	Z	B	E
M	S	T	I	N	I	T	I	A	T	I	V	E	T
Y	N	U	E	E	O	I	I	N	T	I	S	O	
E	L	R	P	I	S	O	L	A	T	E	L	B	F
I	M	L	I	A	I	S	E	E	T	I	B	T	A
F	I	B	R	S	T	U	F	S	A	O	C	U	C
T	E	L	E	C	O	N	F	E	R	E	N	C	E
I	I	S	M	O	A	N	A	Y	I	B	L	I	I
C	O	M	M	U	N	I	C	A	T	I	O	N	I

Unit 10

A

Ex 1

1 B
2 A
3 C

Ex 2

1 Sam Stevens, Gorin Lindgren
2 Gorin Lindgren
3 Ned Spencer
4 Sam Stevens, Gorin Lindgren

Ex 3

1 a
2 b
3 e
4 f
5 c
6 d

Ex 4

1 If the company had found out that Dorota had lied about her experience, they would have fired her.
2 Sheila wouldn't have got into your car if she had realized how bad you are at driving.
3 If I had known it would get you into trouble, I wouldn't have put you in that situation.
4 Would you have taken the job if you had realized how difficult it would be?
5 If you had seen the job advertisement before the closing date, would you have applied for it?
6 You wouldn't have believed how hard he (has) worked to meet the deadline unless you'd seen him.

B

Ex 1

1 $6.2 million
2 ten years ago
3 friends
4 $2.2 million
5 last year
6 big house, cars
7 family

Ex 2

1 debt
2 lend
3 financial
4 mortgage
5 cash
6 down payment

Ex 3

1 b
2 a
3 c
4 c

Ex 4

1 She should have said 'No'.
2 She should have saved some money.
3 They shouldn't have bought a big house.
4 They should have had a decision-free zone.
5 They should have had financial help.

C

Ex 1

1 c
2 e
3 d
4 a
5 b

Ex 2

1 b
2 c
3 a
4 e
5 f
6 d

Ex 3

make: a mess, a decision, an excuse, a mistake, someone defensive/accountable, someone pay
do: some work, something again, your best, a good job

Ex 4

1 make an excuse
2 did the right thing
3 making a mistake
4 take responsibility
5 blame someone else
6 is at fault

D

Ex 1

Conversation 1: photo C
Conversation 2: photo B
Conversation 3: photo A

Ex 2

Dialogue	1	2	3
Apologize	✓	✓	✓
Give an explanation	✓	✓	✓
Take responsibility		✓	
Not take responsibility	✓		
Show concern	✓	✓	
Offer to put things right		✓	✓
Respond to an apology	✓		✓

Ex 3

1 really sorry about this
2 cause you too many
3 to worry
4 'm so sorry
5 there was nothing I could do about
6 I'll get on to it
7 I'll check what
8 accept our apologies for this
9 worry about

Ex 4

1 to
2 about
3 for
4 about
5 to
6 about

Ex 5

1 mistake
2 error
3 fault
4 complication

E

Ex 1

1 open-minded
2 thoughtful
3 kind
4 wise
5 brave

Ex 2

1 a
2 d
3 b
4 c
5 f
6 e

Ex 3

1 honest
2 consistent
3 rational
4 caring

Ex 4

Score:
1–5: You're extremely honest – the person who loses their money near you is very lucky.
6–10: You look at the situation and then use it to your best advantage, but sometime this means being less than totally honest.
11–15: Honesty isn't your greatest strength. Perhaps you should spend some time thinking about how other people feel.

Unit 11

A

Ex 1

1 T
2 F
3 F
4 T

Ex 2

1 which / that
2 when
3 where
4 who
5 that / which
6 which

Ex 3

Defining:
which was started in 1971
when the US was testing nuclear weapons
where some of the last few sea otters and eagles live
which focuses on global environmental campaigns

Non-defining:
who was one of the founding members
who were not aware of the testing
which is based in the Netherlands

Ex 4

1 I gave you the letter which arrived this morning.
2 Jose works in the charity shop which is on High Street.
3 Oxfam is a charity which is based in Oxford.
4 New Orleans is where David comes from.
5 This is the publicity material which Greenpeace sends out.
6 The chef who won the cooking competition lives in Nice.

Ex 5

Young children who were affected by the worst nuclear accident in history got a holiday near York. The children, **who are from Chernobyl,** visited York as part of a holiday in North Yorkshire. The holiday **which was organized by Friends of Chernobyl's Children,** is for one month. The children from Belarus have an increased risk of cancer from radiation caused by the Chernobyl disaster of 1986, **when a nuclear power station exploded.** The children from Belarus went to a school, **where they were met by the schoolchildren,** for a day of activities.

B

Ex 1
1 confirm
2 post
3 appreciate
4 coordinate
5 hesitate

Ex 2
E, F, B, D, G, C, A

Ex 3
a 3
b 5
c 2
d 1
e 6
f 4

Ex 4
1 Hello Jean
2 Thanks
3 Can you tell me if
4 We all really appreciate
5 See you soon

Ex 5
1 I look forward to seeing you.
2 Thanks in advance.
3 I am writing to confirm that I am available.
4 We look forward to hearing from you.
5 We would be happy to make travel arrangements for you.
6 If you have any questions, please let me know.

C

Ex 1
1 retirement
2 wedding
3 maternity
4 promotion
5 engagement

Ex 2
1 China
2 costumes
3 Adelaide University
4 six years

Ex 3
1 has been making
2 has been working / has worked
3 has organized / has been organizing
4 has been encouraging / is encouraging
5 has been talking
6 has confirmed
7 (has) been working / has worked
8 has been enjoying

Ex 4
1 celebrate
2 career move
3 promotion
4 festival

D

Ex 1
1 gossip
2 socializing
3 enhanced
4 liaise
5 troubleshooting

Ex 2
1 people person
2 contact
3 visibility
4 function
5 circulate

Ex 3
1, 2 and 3 are used

Ex 4
1 I don't think we've met before
2 are you with
3 I knew someone at
4 how do you know
5 I hear she's doing very well
6 what about you
7 perhaps I could help you
8 I'd like to introduce you to a colleague

E

Ex 1
Like physical activities: abseiling, orienteering, paint-balling, play-fighting, mountain-biking
Don't like physical activities: laughter therapy, city hunts

Ex 2
1 b
2 b
3 a
4 c

Ex 3
1 Embarrassment
2 challenge
3 therapy
4 athletic
5 incentive
6 away day

Ex 4
1 clear their minds
2 let off steam
3 stretch my legs

Unit 12

A

Ex 1
b

Ex 2
1 a
2 c

Ex 3
1 had made
2 had made
3 had noticed
4 had done
5 was
6 would

Ex 4
1 would
2 have
3 could
4 had to

Ex 5
1 told
2 say
3 Tell
4 saying

B

Ex 1
actress

Ex 2
1 are you happiest
2 Do you know if this
3 Can you tell me
4 Could you tell me
5 Could you tell me when was

Ex 3
A 3
B 2
C 4
D 5
E 1

Ex 4
1 Do you think you will ever get married? / Could you tell me if you will ever get married?
2 Do you think you will make another film? / Could you tell me if you will make another film?
3 Do you think you would like to act in action movies? / Could you tell me if you would like to act in action movies?
4 Could you tell me where your career began?
5 Could you tell me if you are surprised by the success of your movie?
6 Could you tell me if it is true that you are dating your co-star?

Ex 5

1 sue
2 accuse
3 quit
4 split
5 scandal
6 libel

C

Ex 1

Letter 1:
having a car repaired
getting a refund
Letter 2:
letting an apartment
being threatened

Ex 2

1 rogue trader
2 cash in hand
3 ripped off
4 overcharge
5 refund
6 reputable
7 scam
8 cowboy
9 reported
10 screaming and yelling

Ex 3

1 mess
2 trick
3 refuse
4 urgently

Ex 4

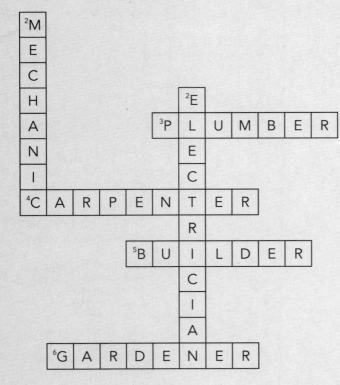

D

Ex 1

1 and 3

Ex 2

1 Jonas Becker
2 812697
3 colour
4 processed
5 replace
6 Yes
7 47455772
8 Bailet
9 battery
10 how much you use the computer
11 website
12 No

Ex 3

1 how may I help you
2 seems to have been a mistake
3 I'm sorry to hear that
4 We've been having some trouble
5 we'll put it right immediately
6 completing our customer feedback questionnaire
7 really very sorry about this
8 If you look at our website

Ex 4

Showing empathy: 3, 8
Apologizing: 2, 6
Correcting and explaining: 5, 7
Putting things right: 1, 4

E

Ex 1

1 pay-per-click (PPC) advertising
2 discussion forum
3 social networking site
4 business angel
5 chat room
6 backer

Ex 2

1 D
2 B
3 C
4 E
5 A
6 G
7 F

Ex 3

1 b
2 c
3 a
4 b
5 c

Ex 4

1 funding
2 determination
3 loyalty
4 maintain
5 update